MW00898952

PLAY THE 1V1 WAY

Soccer Tips from an Emerging Talent Centre

Ian McClurg

Play the 1V1 Way: Soccer Tips from an Emerging Talent Centre

© 2014 Ian McClurg

All rights reserved. No portion of this book may be reproduced, stored in a retrieval system, or transmitted in any form or by any means—electronic, mechanical, photocopy, recording, scanning, or other,—except for brief quotations in critical reviews or articles, without the prior written permission of the publisher.

Every reasonable effort has been made to acquire permission for copyrighted materials used in this book and to acknowledge such permissions accurately. Any errors or omissions called to Ian McClurg attention will be corrected in future printings.

Information on how to obtain copies of this book is available at
www.1v1soccerfc.com

PLAY THE 1V1 WAY:
Soccer Tips from an Emerging Talent Centre

by **Ian McClurg**

Contents

Dedication

It is important for me to say a special thanks to the following people:

To my grandfather and my uncle (Irvine) who ignited my love for the game by taking me to see "the blues" (Linfield FC) on Saturdays.

To my Mum and Dad for their constant love and support.

To my two girls, Olivia and Claudia, for showing me that there are more important things in life than football.

And to my loving wife Shalaina for her daily love and understanding, by letting me do my thing.

Special mention for "my writing coach" Paul Challen for keeping me on track and introducing me to the process of writing a book.

Note: Some of the articles in this book have previously appeared online, at RedNation (www.rednationonline.ca) and Soccer Nation (www.soccernation.com)

I

About the author

Ian McClurg is a UEFA A-licensed coach and head coach/ technical director of 1 v 1 Soccer, based in southwestern Ontario. He founded 1v1 in 2000 to provide young players with the technical skills and game knowledge they need to succeed at all levels of play.

Ian is a former Toronto FC Academy and Ontario Provincial team staff coach, and has worked with 6 players from the current Men's U20 Canadian National team's pool of players and 7 players from the current Canadian Women's National Team.

An avid fan of the game, he also enjoys playing in regular men's league games. He lives in Ancaster, Ontario with his wife, Shalaina, the business manager of 1 v1 soccer, and their children.

Foreword:

What Players, Coaches and Parents Say about Playing the 1v1 Way

COACHES

As an English Category one Academy we are always looking to identify and work with the best players possible, and this includes players in Europe and North America. The 1v1 Soccer Academy is a superb programme that really helps develop players not only technically and tactically, but also socially as well. The coaching programme that 1v1 delivers allows players to work on aspects that we as a Professional Academy are looking for and we really enjoy working with Ian, his coaching staff and more importantly the players that they currently have within the programme. It is refreshing to see so many players develop through the programme over time and we are looking forward to returning to 1v1 soccer Academy in the summer.

Marc Campbell – Lead Foundation Coach,
Wolverhampton Wanderers FC Academy

There are a select few in my humble opinion who take the business of football and football development as seriously and as passionately as my trusted friend and colleague Ian "Cloughie" McClurg, whom I've known for over 15 years. What's even more important to me is that he remains committed to his beliefs and goals that have been mapped out for years. The result? It is not winning or losing, it is far more important than that. It is the development of players, coaches and parents and ultimately the game. There is a dying breed of colleagues such as Ian, who step outside of their own backyard and seek new learning opportunities and outcomes. I'm a huge believer of listen, learn and then lead. Ian magnifies this approach from his own personal and professional development, but also through the development of others. A trusted friend and colleague, a dying breed indeed.

Stuart Neely – Head of Football Development
at New Zealand Football

I have known Ian for many years, from the perspective of a coaching colleague, as a parent lucky enough to have both my children involved as players in the 1v1 family, and as a friend. We have all benefited immensely from our journey with Ian and have been fortunate enough to learn valuable life lessons along the way. Ian's dedication and commitment to the game has been remarkable. Early on, he recognized the importance of developing fundamentally sound technical skills in order to build a solid playing foundation. He was brave enough to change the existing model and was a pioneer in providing age-specific and age-appropriate training methods. He had the courage to strike out on his own, providing meaningful opportunities for players looking to further develop and enhance their game. He has always had the best interest of the player at heart, clearly demonstrated by his player-centred approach. His training content and methods are progressive, setting the highest of standards, all neatly aligned with the top academies in the world. Long may he continue his journey!

Glenn McClung – Ontario Soccer Association instructor/
Technical Director, Hamilton United

Today's modern game of football requires a holistic approach to training so that "the whole" of the individual is developed: body, mind and soul. This is the essential DNA that underlies the 1v1 philosophy as proselytized by Ian McClurg in his new book. Whether you are a passionate lover of the beautiful game or just a passing fan, this guide to soccer development will surely enlighten you and your perceived notions of what works and what doesn't when it comes to developing young players. Ian's expertise in football is first class and his new book will surely become a staple reference on your bookshelf.

Dr. Nick Bontis, Youth Coach and Professor,
McMaster University

PARENTS

You have worked hard Ian with a lot of kids who are now reaping the benefits of higher level soccer. Congrats, and thank you for your continued support and efforts to improve soccer in Canada. You are a first-class coach and one that I would always recommend to others. You are light years ahead of others when it comes to development of young players. Keep up the excellent work.

Mark Roberts

If you want to see quicker results in your children's soccer development then I highly recommend Ian McClurg's 1v1 Academy. The sport-specific training sessions not only cover the playing aspect of the game but Ian has derived a program whereby players are encouraged to develop at all levels including neurological, nutritional and physical. My son, who will be travelling to Europe next year for try outs with European professional clubs, has been attending 1v1's small group sessions for the past 18 months and his player development is beyond even what I had hoped for. With improved agility, co-ordination and strength coupled with Ian's unwavering insistence on personal skill development, it is no surprise that my son's abilities have improved both on the practice and game field.

Pat Malleret

At Ian McClurg's 1v1 Soccer program, top international coaching qualifications, experience and expertise are blended with respect, creativity and a real focus on developing each young soccer player in a comprehensive and holistic way. Players are provided with firm instruction on the tactical and technical skills needed to be proficient but are also encouraged to be creative, express themselves, learn from mistakes and make their own decisions. As a parent of a 1v1 player, what I see is a group of kids who are not only learning to play well but are really enthusiastic about the learning process.

Ben Ratelband

My son Daunte has been training with Ian McClurg's 1v1 soccer program for the past 5 years; he is now almost 11 years old. My intentions for Daunte were to have him be developed by a top rated coach that will bring out the best in my son's abilities. The skills he has learned with Ian have exceeded my expectations and what I like most is the freedom for creativity and positivity from Ian. Ian's strict but fun program has built some core values in my son that will last a lifetime. He enjoys the constant challenges and improving his level of play. Daunte continues to thrive and excel at 1v1 as he works towards a college scholarship or his dream of playing in Europe. Thank you Ian for your continued encouragement and being the great trainer that you are.

Natalie Wruck

I would like to take this opportunity to personally thank Ian McClurg, Director of Coaching at 1v1 Soccer FC. My son, Liam Outlaw, has had the good fortune of being trained and developed under the strict overseeing of Ian for 3 years. Having recently returned from the Danone Nations Cup Finals in London, England, Liam had the opportunity to represent Canada on the international stage. Competing against soccer super powers Brazil, Spain, Argentina, along with several others, Liam was able to match up with the best in the world. Playing as a box-to-box central midfielder, many of Liam's skills, developed and honed at 1v1 Soccer FC, were put on display for the world to see. I am pleased to be associated with Coach McClurg, and would highly recommend his academy and training methodology for soccer players of all ages.

Josh Outlaw

Being a new comer to the world of 1v1, our son's unparalleled drive for this incredible game has been reignited!!! After spending 5 minutes last fall in the skills training class, we knew that this was what learning this game was all about. Thank you for your passion and commitment!

Melanie Lerner

Prior to discovering Academy soccer, both our sons had the opportunity to play locally at the City and/or Rep level. It was quite apparent that key essential aspects of development, discipline and unbiased training were all lacking. Thankfully, it wasn't long before we were introduced to Ian McClurg and 1v1 soccer. We are honoured to have our children be a part of his organization and represent 1v1 in a well-organized SAAC league. As our boys are now beginning their second and third seasons with Ian's program respectively, we can quickly appreciate how the quality of their development, the transition of their mental awareness, their mindset, and the ability for them to predict and read the game are all evolving exponentially and are becoming more natural. Ian's certification level and coaching insight are evident not only on and off the field, but his knowledge of the game becomes transparent almost instantly in every practice and during competitions. In my mind, Mr. McClurg is truly a gentleman, a fantastic coach, and an excellent role model for our family and for the development of basic fundamental skills that will help young players understand and appreciate the world's best sport. His credentials, history in the sport and brilliant resume speak for themselves. Thanks once again to Ian McClurg and the 1v1 staff for making soccer fun again.

Cesare Ciavarro

When Ian McClurg told me he was writing a book on soccer, I was interested but skeptical. As an author of more than 30 books myself, lots of people tell me they're writing one, that's the last I ever hear of it. But, consistent with his approach to soccer (and life in general), Ian got organized and did it. This book has something for everyone interested in developing successful young soccer players – parents, coaches, and of course, the players themselves – wrapped up in Ian's unique philosophy and wit. As the father of two young players committed to "playing the 1 v 1 way" I can recommend this book to anyone who wants an engaging guide to developing better players, and boosting knowledge and passion for the "beautiful game."

Paul Challen

PLAYERS

As a former player of Ian's I will say this: I made his U-14 provincial squad as a striker. He had faith in my skills and taught me from scratch the important position of left back. Being young and wanting to only score goals, I at first objected. But Ian has an eye for skills in young players like no coach I've ever had. Through his coaching and motivation, I was able to make the squad that was sent to the Nationals that year, and started every game at left back. We went on to win gold against Quebec. An experience I will never forget. What I'm saying is this: don't close doors on your child's development because you think they should be at a certain position or they should be playing at a certain age. Ian has only the best interests of your child in mind and wants to see his or her skills develop into full potential.

Meaghan Hughes

As an 11 year old, I have great respect for Coach Ian. He is the best coach primarily for 2 reasons: training and succeeding. He has turned me into a mindful, spiritual, and technical player. I look forward to our trip together to the Wolves elite camp next spring, which under his guidance, I have trained very hard to earn a spot in. Thanks again to my coach for continuously teaching me to be a better player and person.

Matthew Ciavarro

Before working with Ian, I was training with teams that had little or no emphasis on technical soccer. None of my other coaches had the same level of knowledge and/or enthusiasm about the game that Ian brings to each and every session. All of his training is different and challenging, and players learn something new from each one. 1v1 players learn to play a more European-style of soccer (very technical, and not always focused on results) which has really helped me to improve my game. I am looking to play University soccer in the US after high school, and hopefully professionally after that, and Ian's training is putting me on the right course.

Eva Challen

The training is really intense but Ian and the coaches always still find a way to make it fun.

William Ratelband

Ian has played a key role in helping me get closer to my goal of playing overseas. He has shown me the intensity needed to compete at a high level, he has helped me develop a better touch, and has given me opportunities to get exposure in Europe and the US.

Anand Sergeant

1v1 training is a great environment and a great way to work on your skills. I recommend working with Ian to any player looking to improve their skills and further their love of the game.

Henry Challen

INTRODUCTION:
Everything starts with a vision

I started 1v1 Soccer back in 2000, because I felt that there were not enough young players in Ontario receiving quality coaching. The provincial association would choose a small pool of players to train in the provincial programs and, in reality, the programs could only cater to a small number of players within a convenient drive time of the training centre at Vaughan. We aimed to help change that by offering additional training programs to many other young players who were keen to improve but, for one reason or another, found themselves outside the Ontario Provincial teams' programs.

To be honest, though, simply providing additional training programs was not enough for me. My ultimate goal was to be able to develop young players within Canada who could then go on to play soccer at the very highest levels of the game. This could include playing overseas for a professional club, playing for a professional club in North America, playing at a US college on a soccer scholarship or playing for our national or provincial teams. I wanted to develop a training system that could be compared favorably with any other throughout the world. Lofty ambitions, when you're thinking of taking on large, well-established professional soccer institutions like Barcelona, Real Madrid, Arsenal, Manchester United, AC Milan and Juventus! However, you have to start somewhere, and it certainly helps to have many traits of the typical male from Northern Ireland: stubborn, and not in a mood to surrender any time soon!

It also helps to have a clear vision. Many times I have read that it is important to write your goals down as a compass towards your ultimate destination. I would agree with that and have followed this process religiously. Based on my experiences, however, I can hold my hands up and admit that life does get in the way. As well, the politics of youth sports in Canada can drain you, making it very tough to stick to a pre-set plan. And if truth be told, I suppose I have to admit that perhaps I don't really want to find a final destination! To me, a lot of the fun – and most of the challenge—is in the journey. But if I did have to sum up our overall goal at 1 v1, I would borrow the words of the great developer of young players, Dario Gradi at the English club Crewe Alexandra: Our goal is to develop better and better players—and more and more of them!

The ideas I set forward within these pages reflect my experiences as a youth soccer coach in Canada, trying to teach young players technical skills and how to understand the game better. Along the way, I have also always wanted to develop young players as better people. Learning step-overs and juggling isn't enough. You have to also learn to respect the world's greatest game, treat your time playing it like a gift, always strive to be better and always understand that your own conduct is a reflection of yourself and your family. My grandfather, father and uncle all provided me with a great passion for the game and in my own way, I have tried to pass this along to the young players I've come across.

This path has taken a fair amount of time out of my life, and driven those around me a little crazy. But I am hoping that you as a coach, player or parent can benefit from some of the lessons that I have learned, and still continue to learn along the way! In his book *The Talent Code*, author Daniel Coyle—a major influence on my thinking about development—talks about the idea of the "hotbed"; that is, a small geographical area that produces a disproportionate number of very successful people in a given field like sports, music or the arts.

With that in mind, our goal is to have people in the very near future asking why there is a little "soccer hotbed" in southwestern Ontario developing some of the game's greatest

And of course we'd like the answer to be "because there's this great program called 1 v1 Soccer at the heart of it all."

In the pages that follow, I'd like to share with you some of the ways and methods we use—and will continue to use—to fulfill that goal.

PLAY THE 1V1 WAY

Soccer Tips from an Emerging Talent Centre

It's about the player
(Surprise, surprise!)

OK. Let's get something clear right from the kickoff: If we are going to produce successful players, we as coaches and parents must put them at the central point of learning! Our focus, as coaches, must always remain on the technical, tactical, physical and mental development of the individual. Every child that enters any sport's training program must one day leave the program, not only a better player, but more importantly, a better person. The player's academic education must work hand-in-hand with their learning as a player. The top soccer clubs in the world such as Barcelona have long held that manners, values and education are very important components of a young player's development. Now, that approach has to filter down to the grassroots levels of the game.

That may seem obvious. But many coaches and parents seem to think all players are the same, meaning that every young person's development will follow the same path. In my experience and in the experience of many top professional players, that is simply not true. Players learn at different paces, and respond differently to training. Often, human development factors like physical and emotional maturity, rather than pure soccer skills development, influence their status and progress amongst their peers.

It seems that at earlier and earlier ages we are trying to identify talent and make decisions on the level a younger player will reach.. But for the most part, this is not useful. I remember Arsène Wenger, the manager of the great English club Arsenal and one of the best developers of young soccer talent, once stating that if someone looks at a player younger than 14 and tells them you that he or she will become a professional earlier than 14, they are lying. I often relate that quote when talking to parents or other coaches about a player's "future success", because, for many years in the development cycle, you simply can't tell. You see little indications along the way, but never a definite indication of how far young players can go until the age of 16-18.

Over the years, we've all seen many parents who have given up on their children "making it" as young as ages 7-8, and who, after that, no longer support their child's interest in the sport. As well, "playing up" in older age groups becomes the barometer for parents to gauge their child's progress, or as "proof" that their child is succeeding. Coaches are lobbied, competition amongst parents begins, and the end result is that young players are placed under pressure to perform from a very early age.

Many parents have brought their children to our program and instructed us to "make them more aggressive." On such occasions I've taken the "educational" approach and explained that the most important component for all young players is to master the ball, feel comfortable with it and spend time improving basic skills like dribbling, 1v1 moves, turning, passing and shooting. Young players must be placed in situations where they are allowed to try things, use their imagination, and more importantly, enjoy the game and have fun! If they are not enjoying it, guess what? That's right: they are not going to spend any time next week with a ball at their feet!

There have been many of our more skilled players who have participated in skills classes for several years before they've become comfortable in games. One of our young players, aged 6, had a very placid personality and used to run away from the ball and turn his back whenever it came to him. He spent well over a year being very methodical in learning skills such as the step-over but was never confident enough to try the moves playing with others in games. Then all of a sudden, in his own time, he started to do drag-backs, step-overs and go on mazy dribbling runs! What happened? The boy did not change his basic temperament, but because of the confidence that he had developed with the ball, he was now playing at a much higher level. His father, in the early days, had focused on his son's lack of aggression and had asked that we make him more aggressive in 1v1 challenges. But to the father's credit, he had listened to my advice, kept encouraging his son and was able to enjoy watching the boy's progress! It was a classic win-win-win situation — for the player, the parent, and the coach!

The development of a young child cannot be fast-tracked without consequences. It makes little sense, except in rare cases, to have a child jump several grades at school, and it's the same thing for sports development. Nature provides its own built-in development path, and we as soccer coaches have no right to mess with it!

Here's a great example: When the young North Ireland star George Best signed at age 15 for Manchester United in 1961, United's legendary Manger Matt Busby instructed his coaching staff to "let the boy develop naturally." Within two years he was playing in the first team, and within seven years was the best player in European, if not world football! A young Lionel Messi, who emigrated from Argentina to Spain with his family when he was 12, was not "rushed" at Barcelona. Even though he had fantastic talent, he could have likely played for Barca's first team much sooner. But the coaches at the famous La Masia Academy allowed him to progress gradually like the other young boys, and he was provided with the opportunity to develop as a young person, in tandem with his development as a player. And did he develop!

So, let's go back to our first premise — that we need to make sure we keep individual player development at the heart of our coaching efforts. Let's make sure we help our young players grow in all areas, both physical and emotional, and at their own pace. Our job is simply to give them opportunities for that development to happen.

Don't be a slave to team results

The pursuit of winning games and thus promoting teams to higher and higher levels of play, by parents and coaches continues to hold back the progress of Canada at the youth development levels. The Canadian Soccer Association has introduced the philosophy of "long-term development" across the country, yet there is reluctance to abandon the practice of keeping scores, and a continued willingness to measure youth success by the number of wins a team has amassed over its season.

At 1v1, our approach has been to place individual long-term player development for all our players ahead of short-term team development for a select few. This is a philosophy consistent with professional club academies in Europe, where the objective is to educate and develop as many players as possible for higher levels of play. Academy coaches at such legendary teams as Wolves , Arsenal, Liverpool, Manchester United, Barcelona, Real Madrid, Bayern Munich, and Santos do not concern themselves with winning games, and nor should they. What does concern these teams is ensuring that as many of their young players as possible have the skills required to succeed at higher levels of the game in the future.

Many people are surprised that players who grow up playing in successful teams frequently do not reach the higher levels when they leave those strong teams. That's because as they get older, they become more and more dependent on talented players around them. The situation changes when they go on trial at professional clubs overseas. If young players do not develop the ability to overcome adversity during game situations, embrace it and channel it into becoming better, they simply will not be able to play at the highest levels!

But people often ask me, "Doesn't it make sense that a young player in a good team will simply get better and better by training with this team, since the overall strength of the team will pull them up to higher levels?" Not necessarily. I once had a colleague who focused his time on purely building a U12 "super team." The team spent practice after practice running through patterns of play that could be used in games. The players rarely spent any time, even at this young age, developing their individual skills. They went through one entire academy league season undefeated and were rarely challenged by other teams. At that point, my former colleague proudly announced to me that two of the players would go on to play soccer professionally in Europe, two more would play for Canada and all the rest of the squad would be receiving US scholarships! (Remember what Arsène Wenger said about "predictions" like this about players under the age of 14? See page 4 for more on that!)

Don't get me wrong — the team was full of very good players, who played very well together. They kept possession very well, looked always to play attacking football and the players demonstrated great team spirit. They also were very committed to their coach and several families in South Western

Ontario were desperate to join this team and be part of their success in team play. To be sure, that's a team dynamic that any coach would admit is not easy to build and maintain.

However, when 1 or 2 players were taken out of the team, the overall performance slipped dramatically. The strength of the team became greater than the sum of its parts, and performance levels dropped when a few players were missing.

Personally, I feel that players on teams like this, who "stroll" through games easily and do not have experience with different coaches and players, will struggle to reach their full potential. At some point the inevitable happens and they will have to leave the comfort of their long-time team and try to play in another — often higher-level — side. When the "team goals" and results supersede the vision of developing technically excellent and innovative players with exceptional decision-making skills, then I feel that the opportunity for individual development is compromised. Players aged 9-12 must be placed in challenging, stimulating and interesting environments where technical development remains the key consideration. At times, players must "struggle" through this development path and work hard to develop a "thirst" for mastering the ball. Young players must be encouraged to play in several different positions and start to become students of the game!

Time will tell if my evaluation of this particular "super-group" of youngsters is accurate, but in my opinion, it is too early to be thinking of professional contracts, playing for the national team and pursuing US scholarships.

There are just too many training hours and skills to learn before that!

Build your own
from within

A recent documentary on the long-running U.S. news show 60 Minutes provided the soccer world and non-fans alike with a glimpse of what is possible with a long-term development program. The FC Barcelona team in Spain is currently recognized as the best club team in the world and some experts argue the best of all time. What is somewhat unique about their academy model is that one of the world's largest clubs has spent the last 10 years developing their own players in-house. Yes, they have still spent millions of Euros to bring in some of the game's greatest players. But the fact remains that they have also developed 17 out of the 25 players in the current first-team squad within their own La Masia academy. Some of these players, like Cesc Fábregas and Gerard Piqué, have left to join Arsenal and Manchester United, respectively, of the English Premiership, but have now returned back to Barcelona.

A key reason that this team has been so successful is that the current group of players have grown up together and have all been schooled, quite literally, in the Barcelona way. A soccer education is obviously a key component of this program but so also is the academic development of the players. The Barca academy employs teachers to provide lessons in all school curriculum areas, ensuring that the players there receive academic as well as soccer instruction. Several of the players have spoken openly about an almost "telepathic" understanding with their teammates, which has been developed during long hours on the training ground. After Barcelona's win in the Champions' League in 2009, two of the team's midfielders, Xavi and Iniesta, were asked how they managed to string together so many passes together. Iniesta reportedly answered that it was easy, since they'd started doing it when they were 13!

So, what relevance does the Barcelona model have on the grassroots levels of the game here in North America? The most important lessons are, I believe, that coaches and parents must be much more patient in a young player's education. Parents must look at all options for development, evaluate which are best suited for their child, and be patient in their progress. At the moment, I see parents jumping from one program to another on an annual basis, looking for the next and greatest instant vehicle to propel their child to superstardom!

On many occasions, it becomes a case of a parent trying to ensure that their child is getting any advantage possible over their neighbour's child. It also seems that a large amount of time is spent identifying which teams within a 1 hour drive-time are the best at a particular age-group and then ensuring that they get their child on this team, playing with the so-called "best" players. The parent assumes the role of "agent" and places the child, like stage acts, at the next gig! How unsettling would it be for young children to move schools every year, and learn math or English a different way every time? How would Barcelona's top stars of today have developed if their parents had switched back and forth between the academies of Barcelona and its neighbouring club, Espanyol?

Arsenal manager Arsène Wenger once said that if your child is good at piano, then as a parent you would seek out the best teacher that you could afford and place your child there. How is soccer any different? Maybe in North America we have to park our need for instant gratification when it comes to our children's development. Maybe we need to research and find the program that best fits with our child's development requirements. And just maybe we need to be more patient and stress the love of the game over any potential rewards measured in terms of money or fame. In youth sports, money and fame are awarded to the few, and on many occasions those "payoffs" are fleeting. However, soccer does provide many rewards that are underappreciated. It can provide a healthy lifestyle, fun with friends and nothing less than the joy of playing the world's greatest game.

I'm approaching the half-century mark, and willingly spend my time with many others in our over-40 league on a Friday night in pursuit of this passion. Maybe our youth and we as parents are missing this. I have heard many times in life that it makes sense to dedicate yourself to what you enjoy the most. When you work at something you enjoy, the thinking goes, you will be good at it and in turn the rewards will come! I traded the corporate world to pursue a soccer coaching career full-time based on this philosophy...and while the challenges are many, I wouldn't trade what I do for anything!

Maybe it's time for us as youth coaches to pave the way in North America. Educate parents on the benefits of long-term development, provide clear pathways for our players to learn, develop and grow. Provide a wide range of programs that can cater to players of all abilities and ambitions and build development programs based on skills development versus recruitment.

It's time to build it....and they will come!

Youth coaching: One size does not fit all!

It is fair to say that youth soccer development can be a mysterious process. Football (soccer) may be the world's most popular game but truth be told it does lag behind other sports with respect to the application of science and the importance of psychology. England, for example, which hosts the world's most successful league, has only just completed the first review of its youth academy system since 1998! In fairness, though, the academy system under review in England is a massive one. There are 9,000 youth players in England's professional club academy system; all competing for a career at one of the 92 professional clubs and very few of these players will become professional players. Well-known organizations like Liverpool, Everton and Manchester United start looking at players as early as 5 and will assess thousands of players before they make decisions on signing player at the U9 level. (Yes, players — or more accurately, their parents — do sign contracts with clubs for eight year-old players.) Many see this as a process of attrition and "survival of the fittest" to unearth players, rather than following a systematic process of development with a high percentage rate of success. But with so many players competing for so few spots, it is true that clubs can afford to be choosy.

I've seen things change a great deal recently, though. In 2003 I spent ten days at one of England's most successful youth programs, Crewe Alexandra Football Club. The coaching and training was first class, but I did not notice much attention being paid to non-soccer development. That was simply the way things were done ten years ago. However, on a recent visit to England we spent time at our partner club, Wolves FC. What was evident was a more holistic philosophy towards development. The education of young players has now became a focus, assisting the families with travel arrangements to training and matches is much more prevalent, and the young players are surrounded by a support staff which include nutritionists, video analysts, fitness professionals and welfare and educational officers!

Wolves FC recently received its Category 1 designation from the English Premier League in a recent audit of academy operations. The club now has much more contact time with its players and takes them out of school for one full day each week. Each training hour is logged and performance development is monitored on a much more frequent basis.

With the increased investment comes higher expectations of success. A greater percentage of the Wolves' first team players every year are being developed from within their own academy system, as opposed to recruiting players from other clubs in England or overseas. Currently, 25 percent of their young players within the U18 and U21 academy teams have received first team opportunities, and the goal is to increase this to 40 percent.

Top clubs now have an increased awareness that not all players are the same, in terms of their physical, mental and emotional needs. They go through different stages of physical and emotional growth and all these factors do impact their soccer development. There is now a greater realization that professional club academies have a greater responsibility to the players and their families to assist in overcoming life's obstacles in becoming a professional footballer, rather than sitting back and waiting for the strongest to survive and come out the other side. Many have referred to this out-dated process as a "sausage factory."

This progress is underway at professional clubs throughout the world. But what does it mean for young players and their families that are currently outside this environment? I think it reinforces the fact that young players and their families must be seeking development opportunities where the player's entire needs are taken care of. Do players have a balanced lifestyle? Are they happy? Are their health needs being met? And are they in an environment that is positive, patient and nurturing?

As youth coaches we must continue to educate ourselves on improving all aspects of player development. We must ensure that there are the necessary medical, educational and sports science services available for our young players to thrive and maximize their potential. For parents, the challenge is to locate the environment which delivers this the best. You are, after all, handing over your most valuable possession, for several hours every week!

And that means it's time to ask yourself: Is the person or organization that you are handing your child over to the best qualified to look after him or her?

Listen to their dreams and help provide the pathways of learning

The young players that we coach all have dreams — and of course they should have! When they are young, everything really is possible and we as adults must provide environments where young players dare to dream. Aspiring young Messis should watch the little Argentinian star on television go on mazy dribbles, beat 4 or 5 defenders and stick the ball in the back of the net...and believe that they can do the same!

We as coaches cannot ask for better "coaching demos" than Lionel Messi playing for Barcelona every week. Young players watch him on YouTube and then want to be like him. This is where we come in. Do you as a coach provide an environment where young players can try new moves, without a fear of failure? When I was growing up in Northern Ireland, we would watch games on TV and immediately run out of the house with a ball under our arms to try our countryman George Best's latest move. Children don't play in the street as much nowadays so we as coaches are responsible for facilitating and encouraging this "self-discovery" learning in a more structured environment.

Self-expression should form a major component of our warm-up at every session. Players should be encouraged to show their latest moves, and to challenge themselves to try new things. And we should always make a "big deal" about the players that fall over. Praise them for that! As The Talent Code author Daniel Coyle has mentioned many times in his work, we want youngsters "reaching" and struggling to be on the edge. That's how they get better.

As the players get a little older, around 10 years of age, more competitive opportunities start opening up for them. MLS academies start looking at players as do the more competitive youth clubs. Players at this age can also participate at ID camps hosted by top European clubs. It is a good age for learning as the players are still very open to new ideas, are not afraid to try new things, and generally speaking are like sponges. They also are still young enough to dream big!

In North America it is important to talk openly to these young players about all their options. In more mature soccer nations in Europe the "pathways" are very well mapped out and typically involve trying to get identified by a professional club's academy. In Canada, things are similar but there are fewer options because we have fewer pro teams. There are three professional club MLS Academies in Toronto, Vancouver and Montreal. However, there are also district, regional and provincial program pathways. There are also youth clubs playing in competitive leagues, and private academies like ourselves playing in their own academy leagues.

Parents and players can get quickly overwhelmed with the menu of opportunities and start chasing all of them, often several at once. Then the players start training and playing 6-7 days a week and an important part of their development is being compromised. Time is spent sitting in cars, when the young player should be out on a field, with a ball at their feet, improving their skills and having fun!

Our focus should not be about the next or latest opportunity. The emphasis should only be about getting a young player on a "pathway of learning" to make him or a better player.

If we can do that as coaches and keep the focus on learning versus the "achievement" of whether they have been selected for the district team, regional team or an MLS academy, then we are doing what is truly best for young players and their families. The greatest achievement for young players in soccer is simply getting better at it! There is no better gift that we as coaches can give our players than that.

Understand a young player's dreams, help make him or her better, and put them on pathways to get better every day. Good opportunities will then find them. It's important to remember that the player does have a certain advantage in this scenario, because every team, after all, is looking to find good players.

Just be confident that the players that you have developed will have good things come to them!

The power of improvisation

As coaches, we are all trained on the importance of planning and organization. When I first started coaching, I would typically write a training session plan on a Monday night and revise it numerous times between then and Saturday's training. To deliver a good session, I thought, I simply had to follow this process. But while I was in this plan-revise-deliver mode, I often marvelled at the more experienced coaches that I worked with, who seemed to simply turn up and deliver a high-quality training session. What I've learned since then, though, is that far from being unprepared, these coaches were just following a different path — one that combined preparation with improvisation.

I'm not advocating that we as coaches should ever consider compromising our core principles of planning and organization. What I now firmly believe, though, is that we should be more flexible and open to trying new things during a training session and a little more in-tune with the unique dynamics of the environment that we are teaching in, a little more in touch with "coaching in the moment." For all your planning and organization as a coach, you really cannot know for sure the mindset of the players until you arrive at the session and observe the warm-up and even the players' body language as they walk into the training facility. You also don't know how their technical touch will be that day. Who knows, maybe some, or even many of the players that you are working with are having an off day. Maybe they are not responding as well as you had hoped to the activities that you had planned. For many years, I tried to plan a couple of alternative activities in mind for these occasions. I still do that to this day (old habits are hard to break) but what has changed is that I'm more trusting of myself to take a training session, where it needs to go.

Again, at face value this appears a little reckless as it does contradict the core coaching principles of planning and organization. But like those experienced coaches I used to observe, I do stick to my planned topic but on many occasions add a new core move into the warm-up, after observing the players for a few minutes doing other warm-up moves. I might notice something that they are struggling with. For example, maybe a player's touches on the outside of the feet aren't working as well as usual, so I will add a couple of new moves or combinations of moves that I've never previously introduced to help them through the rough patch. Recently, I turned up at session with a plan to work on passing, noticed the gym had 8 long benches and randomly placed these around the gym and re-designed my session on the fly to incorporate the benches as passing walls.

These ideas are like little light-bulbs going off in your head. At first, I was reluctant to introduce them as I had never really thought of them before and felt they needed further analysis. Now, I trust myself enough, to incorporate them into a session and document them later, noting the specifics of the change, and whether or not they worked. The "trust-yourself" model works like this: You have a spontaneous idea in the moment, standing on the field with the players. It seems to make sense at the time and seems to fit in nicely with the flow of the session. My advice is start believing you've made the right call — after all you know your players and you know the game. You then go back later and assess what worked and what didn't, and you keep the "good stuff" for later use.

This approach is completely consistent with how I've argued we should teach players to solve problems themselves on the pitch, and not as coaches constantly telling them what to do. At 1v1 we ask players to use their imagination, try new things and be prepared to make mistakes during training. We as coaches can ask the same of ourselves and push the limits of our coaching abilities.

Coaching is, at least according to the "formal" definition, a teaching, training or development process in which an individual receives support while learning to achieve a specific personal or professional result or goal. Further that process by being innovative and trying new things when providing support to your players. They will thank you for it because their learning will be fun, spontaneous and more enjoyable.

And you will grow massively as a coach.

If they can't learn, they can't play

I'm very fortunate to have a lovely wife who frequently asks me if I realize what I've achieved or that I'm good at what I do. My typical response is short, to-the-point and it constantly baffles her. I simply answer no and move on. The reason is simple: I don't want to think about it. I just want to focus on how to improve our level of training. I'm from a culture where you put your head down and get your job done to the best of your abilities. When you grow up in Northern Ireland there is no time for "big time Charlies" (being big-headed) and if you do go down that path, there are enough people around to snap you back into place very quickly.

I would not have swapped my upbringing for anything. I've seen enough arrogant people in professional and youth soccer to know that you never stop learning. If you ever think you've cracked it, the game itself has a habit of reminding you how much more you have to learn. In a recent interview with the soccer site RedNation Online, I was asked a couple of very good questions.

The first question was: what are the biggest challenges that young Canadian players face when competing with players from other countries for professional playing opportunities? And the second question was: what do we have to do to produce young players at the highest levels of the game? (You can read the full interview at *www. RedNationOnline.ca*)

I weighed up the questions very carefully before I answered because I've often debated these questions in my own head. My mind wandered back to my own time sitting in a changing room at the English club Swindon Town back in the 1980s. I never played professional football but did think I could. (Just in case you are wondering — I had traveled to Swindon on a trial in the 1980s and left after 10 days injured and not believing that I had shown my best. The same injuries would prevent me from training or playing much for the next two years and the opportunity was gone.) It then flashed forward to a few months ago when as a coach I travelled to observe the Wolves FC academy system in the UK. Finally, I thought about a book I've recently finished called *Family, Life, Death and Football: A Year on the Frontline with a Proper Club* by Michael Clavin, that detailed just how hard it is to "make it" as a professional player, and the determination and good fortune that have to accompany that journey.

With all that in mind, my answer to the first question was that the biggest challenge that faces young Canadian players when competing against the world's best is mental strength.

Young Canadian players, like Owen Hargreaves of Calgary, have left home at a very young age, moved to a foreign country without their family, plunged into a different culture without understanding the language, and yet have found the strength within themselves to perform at a higher level than the young "home-grown" players around them. In Owen's case, he was certainly talented technically, physically and tactically but that was not enough in the competitive world he had moved to in Germany. He had to have the strength of character to battle through the challenges he faced at Bayern Munich, one of the world's greatest clubs. He put his head down, worked hard and refused to give up.

Hargreaves was open to learning, and did not start believing he had "made it" already at 13 when Bayern came knocking on his door. I'm sure he was very proud that a top European club had identified and selected him but he did not see his selection as a final destination — rather, he took it as a great opportunity to work harder and achieve even more. He took full advantage of that opportunity to eventually win a Champions League Medal and play for England. (His father was English and therefore Owen chose to play for that country rather than Canada.)

Contrast that with what I've seen at the Toronto FC academy when I worked there as a coach: young players with the latest multi-coloured Nike boots with their initials sewed into them. That may seem like a minor thing, but it sends a clear signal about what the players, their families, and even the team consider to be truly important. At Wolves FC, however, the academy boys are required to wear black boots. It is a little reminder that they have yet to achieve anything and to — literally! — keep their feet on the ground and keep learning.

The answer to the second question was quite simple. What we in Canada need to do to produce more top players who can compete on a world level is to keep our young players humble. They should be open to listening, prepared to work hard and if professional football (soccer) is their end goal they must understand the mental strength and resilience required in order to earn the right to play and remain at that level.

I think the final word on this should go to the Australian writer Robert Hughes who — though I am not sure was ever a soccer fan — summed it up best when he said:

"The greater the artist, the greater the doubt; perfect confidence is granted to the less talented as a consolation prize."

Futsal: Let the game be the coach!

Futsal — the sped-up, compressed indoor version of soccer (football) — has played an important role in my development work with players during the last four years. Futsal has always been lauded for its role in helping to develop many of Brazil's soccer stars during the last 40 years and the word "futsal" is actually short for "futbal de salao," a term coined in Brazil which roughly means "football in a gym."

As well, the recent emergence of Spain as a dominant soccer nation has highlighted this further, as Spanish stars like Xavi have credited the indoor game for their success. Other legends like Messi, Zidane, Zico, Ronaldo and Iniesta all cite futsal as the source of much of their skills and technical development. (And for a real treat, look up the Brazilian Falcao on YouTube — a futsal specialist who most observers consider the world's best at the game.)

From an individual-player point of view, using the smaller and low-bounce futsal ball in our training classes has greatly accelerated the technical development rate of all our younger players. The ball does not bounce away and makes it easier to learn new skills using all parts of both feet. The heavier weight of the ball also ensures that players have to lock their ankle and use good technique for quick passing and shooting. We have seen a great improvement in the dribbling skills, 1v1 moves, passing skills and shooting of our players during futsal training classes.

It is in tactical areas of the game, however, that I can see the greatest benefits of futsal as a learning tool for young North American players. My generation grew up playing soccer in the streets where space was tight, competition was fierce and you had to be strong mentally to impose yourself on the game and demand the ball. That was because everyone wanted the ball and would do almost anything to get it. It is fair to say that everyone soon learned to execute quality first touches and quick changes in direction and pace, to avoid being caught by flying tackles from a few players who off the field you considered as mates.

Our younger players in North America today do not play in the streets. Instead, they come to organized soccer practices to learn the game and futsal is a great way for us as coaches to accelerate their soccer learning. Futsal places young players in tight spaces (like the school playground or street) and demands from them good ball control, quick thinking, precise passing and creative solutions to get themselves out of tight spaces to create goal-scoring opportunities. Like basketball, there are constant transitions between attack and defence. This provides our young players with many opportunities to face these situations, and these repetitions are an important element of the modern game.

This fall and winter [2012-13], 1v1 Soccer FC is playing in a futsal league in Toronto. This is our first year entering teams in formal futsal leagues and the experience has been very challenging but also very beneficial. Many parents have asked me why I have not provided much coaching direction to the players during games, and why I am not overly concerned with the game scores and competitive results. The reason is simple: The players are learning every minute they are on the field. The speed of the game dictates that the players process information quicker and the feedback is instant: You make an incorrect decision, play a bad pass or cannot control the ball and the opposition now have the ball close to your goal or worse....the ball is in the back of your own net already!

Daniel Coyle in *The Talent Code* speaks of skateboarders being super-quick learners. That's because if they make a mistake, they typically fall (instantly), and immediately gain feedback on what went wrong. So too the life of a futsal player.

It is on occasions like this that we as coaches can do more by doing less. By challenging our players and trusting them to discover the right solutions, we are putting the burden on the player to think for him- or herself. If a player cannot get around a defender, or an opponent is constantly getting around them all the time in a game, we as coaches and parents have to ask ourselves: Are our young players thinking of solutions? Or are they always looking to you as a coach or their parents in the stands?

In my opinion our young players know the game better than we give them credit for — or in fact, better than they give themselves credit for. Of course as adults we need to be there for discussion and to help guide young players towards solutions, but we must be helping our young players think for themselves.

We all want to develop "thinking players." That can only be achieved if we provide an environment where they can practice the ability to try things, perhaps fail at them, and then come up with a solution that works — on their own. Players don't, for example, learn passing by adults drawing diagrams on a white board. They learn the skill by actually doing it. And, as I hope is clear by now, keeping score — and simply "playing to win" in games like the ones we contest in the Toronto league

— is completely irrelevant to the kind of learning we're trying to foster.

Sorry coaches, but despite all our efforts, the game remains the greatest teacher.

If you are in any doubt, consider this: After a tough futsal league game last Saturday, where I sat in the stands and other staff coached the players during the U11 and U14 games, I asked the players to complete a simple task at training the following morning. I asked them to write down three things that they had learned from the game they played less than 24 hours previously.

The responses were as follows:

- Move the ball quicker
- Communicate earlier
- Make your decision before you get the ball
- Be faster
- Get open (move a lot)
- Take shots when close to net
- Decide early (pass, shoot, dribble)
- Talk more, give directions to teammates
- Look for open space
- You have to make quick decisions
- You have to know where and what you are going to do with the ball
- You can't be standing still, you have to keep moving
- Communication
- Fast pace
- Lots of touches on ball

Job done. They already had all the answers. And the best part: I didn't tell them any of it. The game did!

Train in chaos...
Soccer is random

The game of football (soccer) is random. The field and goalposts stay fixed, the lines on the pitch don't move, and the ball is round — but that's about it. Other than that, things are pretty chaotic. The ball moves, teammates are all over the place and so are the opposition. Players have to make decisions in milliseconds, and we as coaches and parents expect them to make these decisions correctly and to execute on them successfully.

Soccer might be a simple game, but it is very difficult to play it in a simple way.

We as coaches stress the importance of young players learning good technical skills. However, it is also very important that we equip them with the tools to process information — both quickly and correctly. So how can we as coaches help our players to learn to cope with the game's challenges? If the game is random, then we must train in a random way. A key component of our training is practicing in very tight spaces with lots of players making turns and executing moves close to each other. Our typical warm-up involves as many as 28 players dribbling and executing moves at game pace within a tennis-court-sized area. Players must learn to keep their heads up to find space to move into or they receive instant feedback: a heavy collision with a teammate. They quickly get used to having many players around them, in tight spaces and they must constantly control and navigate their ball away from trouble. This experience mirrors the real challenges they face when playing the game. For them, it's best to learn how to cope with these challenges in practice, on a regular basis. The old cliché that "if you can't do it in training, you won't be able to do it in a game" is absolutely true in this case.

Those often-seen line drills, while very effective at teaching basic skills through repetition, do little to help our young players cope with the chaos of the game. They may, in fact, be partly to blame for our players at later ages thinking and playing in straight lines, rather than seeing all the possibilities that can open up during a chaotic match.

I remember hearing a story about Franz Beckenbauer, the great German player who many consider one of the top-five players of all time, and the leader of the team who won the 1974 World Cup. (See page 178 for more on Beckenbauer.) Apparently, "Der Kaiser" once stated that at any given time during a game, he could stop, close his eyes and tell you exactly where all his teammates were positioned. The story has resulted in me telling as many of my players who will listen: take a mental picture, all of the time, when you're playing the game. When I don't see them doing that, I sometimes stop practice and ask them to close their eyes and tell me where players around them are located.

As young as age 5, I have challenged young players to learn to cope with the chaos and randomness of the game. Our training is done in small spaces where players must look around constantly to navigate around others in tight spaces. We use four-goal games to get young players used to looking up and deciding what space to move into. We'll then place different coloured pinnies on the goals to encourage quick thinking (i.e. dribble and score in the blue goal) and later on we'll increase the challenge by forcing them to process information quickly.

For example, we'll tell them that when we yell "red pinnies" that really means "shoot for the blue goal" and vice versa. Little things like this can add more fun and enjoyment to practices but more importantly, can teach young players, from as early as age 5, how to process information and make correct decisions.

When players advance, we can then add multiple balls to passing drills and have multiple players dribbling through small grids executing 1v1 moves. In games, we can ask one team to play a passing game (2-touch maximum) and have the other team to play with unlimited touches and take players on in 1v1 situations. Switching these roles back and forth is challenging for the players but encourages them to develop and use assessment and decision-making skills during random movements.

If you really want to add chaos to your practices, ask players to juggle tennis balls with their hands while dribbling or passing. This concept was introduced to me during my UEFA A license course in Belfast and we've tried it with our players. The theory behind it is that by overloading the players mentally, the real game will seem easier to them later on.

Recently, I read an article about a youth coach called Dan Micciche at the MK Dons academy in England. He is really challenging his players by playing 9v9 and then 11v11 games in small condensed playing areas (60 x 40 yds). He even goes a step further by adding in offside areas to further condense the play. The reason for this? He feels that young English players are not talented enough to be able to work successfully in tight spaces. In his sessions, Micciche limits space and time, and to survive in this type of game, you really have to be able to play.

Micciche went on to say that many coaches don't like limiting space because it looks messy. "Sometimes it does because we're asking a lot technically," he admitted to the UK's Daily Mail. "You might not always get quality, but when you do it is the highest quality. And when they go out onto a full-size pitch again, it feels as if they have got all the time in the world."

Try your own methods of adding chaos to training sessions. Challenge players to look around, assess (think), make good decisions and then execute. You will then have developed quick-thinking players who are always one or more steps ahead of their opponents in movements off the ball and their execution on it.

There's only one metric for youth development

Today in soccer (football) we are bombarded with statistics. At our fingertips, Web sites like Four Four Two magazine's "Stats Zone" provides us with possession percentages by each team, pass completion rates by individual players and graph lines illustrating the patterns of play by both teams over the course of 90 minutes.

Youth coaches can also get caught up in measurement. When I became head coach of a large youth club in 2002, I was shocked that many of the coaches were using the beep test — a popular measurement of aerobic capacity. I believed we should have been emphasizing developing the players' technical skills, rather than focusing on physical attributes at such a young age. Today, many youth coaches send players to sports science experts to measure balance (or lack thereof) and other physical attributes. At 1v1 Soccer FC , we ourselves measure the technical ability of players using the iSoccer testing program. Technological advances with iPhones and iPads, and the explosion of coaching apps make it easier than ever before to measure youth soccer performance of teams and individuals. We even have micro-chips in the shoes of young players to measure the distance they covered during games.

To be sure, there is something very definite about numbers that makes us as humans much more confident in our analysis and decision-making. But how should this impact us all as youth development coaches?

My own feeling is that if we can use testing programs such as iSoccer to have players focus on their own individual skill improvements versus the results of games, that can be a good thing. Similarly, greater access to video recording can allow coaches to provide instant feedback to the players on the training field — who may have no idea of what they "look like" when playing — and help to refine and improve technique. Video can also be used as a teaching tool to illustrate decision-making options and assist players to understand the game better.

But there is only one metric that youth coaches should be concerned about: Are your players happy to come back to the next session? When mentoring less experienced coaches I stress this role above all others. We have to provide young players with a fun, stimulating and learning environment that they look forward to participating in. Soccer today is big business but we can easily lose sight of the fact that it is a game. When players come to training, no matter what their age, it is their play time. They don't have to figure our algebra, study literature or be expected to name all 50 states. The training should be challenging, at a high tempo, and should mirror game-like situations where players have to come up with solutions. The goal of a youth coach is to provide an environment where players actually enjoy improving their skills and build a thirst for learning the game more so they can play it at a higher level.

There can be no greater reward for a youth coach than seeing young players leave practice with a smile on their face and turn up for the next practice early eager to learn more. That should be our reference point for knowing that we are doing a good job and helping our young players enjoy the world's greatest game.

You can't graph that. But then again, you don't have to.

Sometimes the best thing you can say is nothing at all

My grandfather was forever offering me the advice that forms this chapter's title as a way to successfully navigate through the dangerous waters of relationships with the opposite sex. On many occasions I wished that I had followed it, because it has powerful applications to just about any aspect of life.

As youth coaches, the recommendation to say nothing can have an important impact on the quality of your work, and the relationships you build with players. Soccer is an emotional game and the pace of the game is very quick. It is challenging for coaches to observe a phase of play in a game or players learning new techniques in practice. Within seconds we are required to analyze what happened, think of all possible ways to help the player or players, decide upon the best solution and then deliver the information in a manner that will make sense to the player or players involved. On many occasions, the information will have to be presented in a way that factors in the specific personality of the player, whether their confidence is currently high or low and the length of time the player or players can take to make any necessary changes to their current performance levels. If they are in the middle of a game, they will have to process this information as the game continues, while during practice the coach will have the option of spending a greater amount of time explaining. And after a game, a coach is often challenged with presenting this just-processed information to a young player and his or her parent, often in an emotionally-charged atmosphere.

As coaches, we are conditioned to — and many would say addicted to — fixing things. We cannot and should not try to fix everything as this approach will only serve to continually interrupt the natural flow of a game or practice. Constant correction can also de-motivate the players by focusing only on the negative. Good coaches will learn through experience to register and bank observations and communicate these at the appropriate moment and in a manner that will lead the player or the players towards performance improvements. If you are not sure about an observation, don't know the correct ways to help a player, and have any doubts on whether to highlight your concerns immediately, then it is best to log the information, hold off on making your views known right away, and give it some additional thought later. It is rare that a player — or parent — won't want to take the time for a chat a day or two afterwards.

This is true at all levels of the coaching profession. Currently, I'm reading a biography on Barcelona's former coach Pep Guardiola by Guillem Balague, subtitled, revealingly, "Another Way of Winning." The book highlights Guardiola's strong abilities as a player, coach and person in listening and observing. During his days building the Messi-inspired Barca team that won 13 out of a possible 16 competitions within a four-year period, Pep would frequently wander around the training ground listening and observing, more than instructing. We can do the same with our young players. Rather than overload them with information, an alternative is to provide them with a training environment that guides them through "self-discovery" to arrive at the correct solutions.

We constantly ask our players to try changing behaviors in order to arrive at performance improvements. This is one challenge that we as coaches can take on board. We need to try it and see if we can become better at what we do. From my own experiences it can take a bit of practice but it does improve you as a coach — and that can only help your players, too.

Think!

An important part of the 1v1 Soccer FC training philosophy is our focus on developing individual skills. It is our belief that all players must have a strong foundation of technical skills before they can advance to playing at higher levels. You can advance your young players even further by including other elements from the "4 corner" model of youth development — combining technical skill development with physical, psychological and social enhancements — during your training activities.

At the young ages we should begin to teach players the importance of problem solving and coming up with solutions during soccer activities. We must get away from technical training as simply a repetition of skills without thought. Learning and enhancing core skills should not be seen as a "drill," which lasts for a specific amount of time before players move on to more enjoyable phases of the practice. As coaches, we can be creative during this type of work and add other elements to technical skills training that can stimulate the players more, and begin to teach them decision-making and what they do in tandem with their teammates.

Although it may sound obvious, a big challenge that we encounter as coaches is teaching young players how to think. The generation we currently coach have grown up with adult-organized "play dates" (a concept totally foreign to someone who grew up in Northern Ireland during the 1970s) and organized and structured youth sports. Young players simply have not been put in situations where they have to think for themselves. Instead, they rely on parents to organize their play, and we as coaches have the responsibility of making them better players in this model.

At 1v1, our philosophy is that if you want young players to take responsibility on the field, and to think and make decisions during the chaos of a game, you have to provide them with more opportunities to practice this when you have contact time with them. See page 170 for more on the positive aspects of soccer "chaos." You also have to take away the element of fear within them for making the wrong decisions. You want to foster creative thinking without the risk of failure.

There are many things that you can do during practice to stimulate and encourage thinking. During technical warm-up work you can separate the field into four quadrants and set the condition that as players move around and execute technical moves, the number of players working in each quadrant must remain the same. Every player is assigned this responsibility and in addition to making sure that their heads are up they are making decisions where to move, based on the movement of the entire group of players surrounding them. In passing exercises, where you want to use repetition for skills improvement, you can have players working in pairs but with the condition that they can switch off partners at any time. Once one player leaves their partner and moves to another partner, the entire group must react to this and made decisions on where to move. To make good decisions with these types of conditions, the players must lift their heads up and see the entire group of players while at the same time executing technical skills such as passing. This replicates game situations where we encourage all our players to view the entire field beyond the ball and their immediate opponents so they can get a wider perspective on the overall play.

This type of work can be extended to small-sided games at the end of practice by giving certain players specific roles. For example, you can tell the striker to drift wide, stay outside the line of sight of defenders and switch wings regularly to keep defenders guessing. By introducing this condition, you can quickly learn the abilities of the defenders to access situations and make decisions with respect to forwards. Did they recognize a pattern with the forward's movements and did they change how they played, based upon that? You can also learn the ability of the forward to understand the role, read the movements of the defenders and to take advantage of their positioning.

It is important in situations like this to remind players and parents that the overall goal is not for a small-sided team to "win" the training matches, but to work on important technical aspects of the game that will come in handy in an actual match.

Soccer, at its most basic, is a series of 1v1 situations all over the field. Are your players equipped to make better decisions than their opponents and are they capable of maximizing their technical skills against opponents? By developing their thinking skills, your players will enjoy greater success.

Tough times teach the best lessons

Coaching soccer is a very rewarding but it can also be a very demanding role. Former players who have taken on coaching roles speak about the challenges of changing their mindset from a single-minded focus on their own needs to all of sudden catering to the demands of an entire group of players. With groups come different aims and objectives, different personalities, different learning methods and ultimately different behaviors. The life of a coach can be simple when things are going well and complicated when they are not going so well.

Most of us who choose coaching as a profession find it a lonely existence and all-consuming. (But of course we would not trade it for anything!) It is rare that your mind fully shuts off and your thoughts are not drifting to the last training session, how certain players are developing, the challenges the group faced in the last game and what you should be working on next week.

What I have learned is that during the down times when you feel that the players are not responding or developing as fast as you would like, you actually make your greatest strides as a coach. That is when you look at everything. You assess yourself as a coach, the training you provide and whether you have communicated your learning in the correct manner. It is not a pleasant process to go through, but an invaluable one for any coach. The trick is to take your time with the process, be patient with yourself and try not to make hasty decisions. The answers will come … and they may take more than one or two sleepless nights to arrive.

Recently, I went through this process. Our younger team (U11s) had struggled during a futsal game. The effort was there from the players but I felt that they had not demonstrated their true technical ability. They could not keep possession in the game and struggled to put three or four quality passes together. They had no pattern to their play and were not communicating. The players were making late decisions when the ball arrived at their feet and they were soundly beaten in 1v1 situations, which contributed to five of the goals scored against us. I had watched the game from the stands which gave me an opportunity to get a better view of the game but I was deflated by our performance, even though it was against a very good team.

At times like this, players, parents and the rest of the coaching staff look directly at you. The players were looking for me to say something so I went to the changing room. Basically, I told them that their effort could not be questioned, that they had all done something well during the game but there were some areas that we needed to work on before the game the following week. I spoke about our need to understand the game better, assess situations and make decisions quicker while developing the mental strength to be more competitive in 1v1 situations. I spoke about helping ourselves a little more through greater communication and that there were some players (2 in particular) who were playing for themselves rather than assisting the team. And, perhaps most importantly, I assured them that they all had the ability to make these improvements and that we would put the work in during the following week of training.

The discussion in the changing room was intended to have the players understand that they could do better. However, I didn't want them to be down to the point that they would shut down and not be open to new ideas during the following week's training. In these types of situations, the sandwich method works well. This is where you as a coach "sandwich" a slice of praise between a piece of criticism and a suggested course of improvement. I praised them for their efforts, identified areas that we could improve upon as a group and then provided a solution as a course of action — we all had the ability to work together the following week to get better.

The message was clear: The players had lots to do, the coaching staff was behind them all the way, and we would need the players to be focused and open to learning for the following week.

After addressing the group, my mind went into overdrive. Was the training preparation good enough? What areas had each player done well in and what areas had they struggled with? Did they read the game and look to find individual and group solutions? How much of the performance was down to how well the other team had played? What was the attitude of the group like prior to and during the game? Were my expectations from the players too high for their age? What were the thoughts of the other coaches? Where we providing them with the tools they needed to succeed in the standard of competition we were playing in? (And yes, I realize — that is a lot of questions!)

This process lasted two full days. It allowed me to review where the group was at in terms of their overall development. Without deviating from our long-term development model, the players required greater assistance from the coaches in game understanding. The following week's training was focused on that. Our players needed greater help in understanding their attacking responsibilities when we had the ball and their defending responsibilities when we had just lost the ball. Futsal can be an unforgiving game when players do not react quickly in these situations.

I'm pleased to report that the performance was much improved the following week. In addition, the experience was a good one for me to clarify what we were doing well in our program and some areas that we needed to work on.

So just remember: Just like in all aspects of life, in coaching, you learn more when things don't go quite so well.

Technique+
Game Intelligence
= Success

As young players advance in the game, it is important that they start learning game intelligence and combining this with technique. When they start playing at ages as young as 4 or 5 the more athletic and skillful players enjoy early success at simply running with the ball and going past players either with skillful moves or sheer speed and determination. They are too young at that age to think about sharing so their runs with the ball generally have two outcomes — they run into a mass of opposing players and lose the ball or they end up scoring a goal. Unfortunately, due to the prevailing attitude of many well-intentioned coaches and parents, goal-scoring in this scenario is considered the only way to measure success on the soccer field, so it is rewarded and praised without proper attention being given to other technical aspects of the game.

Between the ages of 6-10 young players should learn and experience group behavior. It is an important step for them socially to help others around them and accept being helped by others. During this stage of development they should also begin to understand sticking to assigned areas of the field and the importance of being rotated through different positions so that they begin to learn all aspects of the game. Again, within the model of measuring improvement solely via goal-scoring as described above, being assigned a defensive role on a team is often seen as a "punishment" or "a place to put weak players." As coaches we need to fight against this.

Around the same age, however, we begin to see pronounced differences in the technical ability of players, and funneling these players into more elite programs. Personally, I believe that this is too young, but certainly in North America it is at this age that young players begin to receive additional training and the first separation from their peers via the streaming process of "rep" and "select" takes place.

But what qualities do the world's top clubs look for when evaluating young players? They generally begin to consider players as young as 7 but cannot invite them into formal training programs until the U9 level (that is, at the age of 8). Spain has been the leader in recent years with respect to youth development. During my trip to the top-flight Spanish club Sevilla FC in 2011 they confirmed that they look initially for good technique and pace. They then look for young players who understand the game. On the field, are these kids looking around at all their options? Can they make intelligent runs into open space? Can they make correct choices when to dribble and when to combine with teammates? These same qualities are highly prized by our partner club in the UK, Wolves FC, although they will generally pay greater intention to the physical characteristics of players, as in England the physical demands on players are generally much higher than in Spain.

According to the English FA's Technical Guide for Young Player Development — The Future Game, young players of the future will be required to release the ball accurately and instantly over a variety of distances using both feet and on any surface. A quality first touch will be critical as will the ability to operate successfully in congested areas with speed and precision. Retaining possession will be a key feature of play for Elite players and so will possessing the "craft" to disguise techniques and "out-smart" their direct opponents.

The ability to exchange passes quickly and accurately with teammates on a consistent basis will increase in importance as a player gets older, rather than repeatedly taking players on in 1v1 attacking situations. As players mature they will have to demonstrate their ability to decide what to do and when to do it within the demands of game situations.

If all of this sounds like too much "theory" just consider the success in recent years of the Spanish national men's team — winners of the 2008 and 2012 European Championships and the 2010 World Cup. Every player on the team, regardless of his position, has a flawless first touch, knows how to move the ball quickly, makes sound, quick decisions in all phases of the game and is willing to combine all these qualities with his teammates to form a team that is the only one in soccer history to have won three major titles in a row.

Taking all these factors into consideration, we have put technique at the cornerstone of all our programs. Good technique is a base requirement but what will really determine how far our players will go will be their ability to consistently make the right choices and create solutions on the field. A key reason I watch our Futsal games from the stands and watch video of the games is to evaluate how well the group and individual players are progressing with this. It can be an overlooked area of players' development but it is a vital one.

A combination of good technique and game intelligence can take our young players to higher levels of the game. I often tell the tale of Pep Guardiola being chosen for Barcelona — the club team that has supplied most of the players to the Spanish national side — as a skinny, slowish youngster because of his leadership qualities and game intelligence which far outweighed his speed and or other physical attributes at an early age.

Apparently his career in the game worked out rather well in the end!

How much time should young players spend with the ball?

Arsenal manager Arsène Wenger may, over the past few years, have come under considerable criticism for first team results. But most observers of the game agree that since arriving at the North London club in 1996, he has established the "Gunners" as a world leader in youth development. Out of the last 100 players that have made their debut for the first team, 49 have progressed through the Arsenal Academy.

Rather than spend $60 million dollars a year on players like Manchester United, Chelsea and Manchester City, the club has increasingly developed its own players. The advantage of this model is that the players have a greater loyalty and affiliation to the club and tend to stay longer. In addition, they can be schooled from a very early age to play "The Arsenal Way." Not all the Arsenal youth players have or will graduate to the first team but they will have a great chance at becoming professional players, at some level.

From 1v1 Soccer FC's perspective, the Arsenal model confirms our belief that for players to become successful in the game, they must be practicing more and more with the ball. Steve Bould (former Arsenal defensive star as a player, current assistant manager and former youth team coach) believes that young English players are still behind young European players in terms of weekly training time.

"It's hard because I look at Spain, France or Holland and the kids are training four, five or six times per week at young ages," says Bould. "At 15 we get ours three times a week (which includes a game) at the very most."

Looking at another development model in Brazil youngsters also play constantly with the ball, easily 12-15 hours a week, but in a more unstructured environment like pickup games in the street or on the beach. However, it is important to remember that while these players may not have "coaches" in the same we understand the term, there is always an older sibling, parent, relative or friend to pass along lessons of technique and the fundamentals of team play.

The Elite Performance Plan for English clubs, released in 2011, does significantly increase the training contact time that Category 1 clubs now have with young players. Training hours for U9 to U11 players has increased from 4 hours per week to 8, and for U12-U16 players this has been increased from12 hrs per week to 16. Wolves FC, for example, now take their young players out of school one day each week to expand their training.

Consider now the averages for young players in Canada or the US, who may only train once or twice a week, at a low tempo, without a significant technical component while being taught by volunteer coaching staff who have not had the opportunity to spend time learning the game and what is best in terms of youth development. The bottom line is that even when the players do train they may not be spending time on the correct activities.

Arsenal's Bould also highlights another important characteristic that must be combined with greater touches on the ball — character! For players to play at a higher level, they must learn how to overcome adversity and develop skills to overcome "problems" both on and off the field. Daniel Coyle also highlighted this as an important aspect of a child's development in his book The Talent Code. The struggle to master a new skill or to work out how to receive more touches in small-sided games against older or more experienced players is a very important part of development.

No player will be able to instantly juggle the ball 300 times in succession without constant practice. It is the young players that keep practicing and have the belief in themselves that they can achieve a higher level of play — despite any obstacles or setbacks — who will ultimately be successful. That player may not necessarily be the best player today, they may have been told by a coach that they are too small or not aggressive enough. If they keep working on their technical ability and have the determination and passion for the game to be successful, then these types of players will be our best players in future years.

Young Brazilian players are spending 12-15 hours a week working on their ball skills and the young European players are training five or six times each week. Consequently, Canada must adopt the same philosophy towards technical development if we wish to be truly successful in soccer in competition with these nations.

I am frequently asked when Canada will have a successful national men's team. My answer is always the same — 2030. After all, that is when the majority of our 1v1 Soccer FC players will have hit the ideal ages of between 25 and 30!

Attacking skills — the cornerstone of the modern game

At the end of 2012, one weekend in the English Premier League produced the second highest number of goals in the league's 20-year history. Arsenal defeated Newcastle United 7-3, and Manchester City defeated Norwich City 4-3 with 10 men. This followed Chelsea's 8-0 defeat of Aston Villa and Manchester United's 4-3 defeat of Newcastle United during previous weeks.

What is significant is that the top teams in the EPL are placing an increased emphasis on their team attacking options rather than playing with defensive caution. Manchester United quite easily won the 2012/2013 English Premiership League and at the end of 2012 were the leading goal scorers in the league — both at home and away. However, at that time, there were 9 other teams with better defensive records during home games, and 2 other teams with better defensive records during away games. Before the season had even started, Manchester United had signaled their intent to outscore other teams in the league in order to regain their Premiership title by purchasing Robin Van Persie from Arsenal for 24 million pounds, instead of investing in the weaker midfield and defensive areas of their squad.

But it is important to remember that it is not only strikers who play a significant role in a team's attacking play. The majority of teams in the English Premiership typically play with only 1 striker. Therefore, midfield players and full-backs have important roles to play in the attacking phases of play. Brazil has long used attacking full-backs arriving late in wide positions to overload defenders, to generate crosses or create dribbling opportunities into the box for goal-scoring opportunities. In Arsenal's 7-3 win over Newcastle, striker/ winger Theo Walcott scored three goals, and French forward Olivier Giroud potted two goals, yet the Gunners' right full-back Bacary Sagna was involved the most in their attacking play over 90 minutes. Similarly, in Chelsea's 8-0 win over Aston Vila it was the Blues' right full-back, the Spaniard Cesar Azpilicueta, who had the most influence in their attacking play.

It is generally acknowledged that at the top levels of the game, the team with the most possession controls play and as a result typically wins the game. However, statistics confirm that it is the quality of a team's attacking play in the attacking third (rather than quantity of the play) that has a greater influence on results. For example, during Newcastle United's 7-3 defeat to Arsenal they had a greater amount of possession (59 per cent v 44 per cent), attempted a higher number of passes (462 v 340) and achieved a higher pass completion rate (89 per cent v 83 per cent). The difference was that Arsenal completed a greater number of their passes (100 v 68) in the attacking third. The pace and trickery of players such as Walcott and Alex Oxlade -Chamberlain and the quality of their finishing (10 out of 16 shots on target) proved the difference.

Similarly, Chelsea enjoyed 57 per cent of possession versus Aston Villa's 43 per cent and only enjoyed a small advantage over Aston Villa in the percentage of completion of their passes (87 per cent v. 8 per cent). Again, it was the difference in the number of passes completed within the attacking third and the quality of the finishing that resulted in the 8-0 score. Chelsea successfully completed 148 out of 191 of their passes in the attacking third versus Aston Villa's successful completion of 63 out of 107. Fifteen of Chelsea's 26 attempted shots were on target, while Aston Vila only had 1 shot on target, out of their 7 attempts.

Some people may conclude from these statistics that it is the teams that have more play in the opposition's attacking half that typically go on to win games. Therefore, a successful tactic would seem to be simply to get the ball forward quicker. However, this is not supported by game statistics. Arsenal only enjoyed a territory advantage of 54 per cent v 46 per cent versus Newcastle in their 7-3 win and Chelsea only enjoyed a 56 per cent v 46 per cent advantage over Aston Villa in that 8-0 win.

Again, it is the quality of the attacking play in the "final" third that makes the difference. The teams that best control possession in these areas with short 1 and 2 touch passing and penetrating dribbling runs typically create more goal scoring opportunities by pulling well-organized defences out of position.

So, what type of youth training can best prepare our young players for success in the modern game? To be effective in the attacking third of the field requires:

- Good technique in tight areas
- Ability to play quick 1 and 2 touch passes
- Quick thinking to make effective movements off the ball
- Imagination, skill and courage to take players on in 1v1 situations
- Early finishing using both feet

- Ability for quick transition — from defense to attack, and attack to defense

At 1v1 Soccer FC we believe that a combination of futsal training and games is the best development model during the winter months to develop these skills. The play is fast-paced and players are naturally challenged to think quickly, play at a high tempo and to be constantly making effective runs to create space.

The game is changing and we must make the necessary changes within our own youth development training programs to reflect this. Only then can we successfully prepare our players so that they can excel at the highest levels!

Inspiration for those who challenge traditional methods

"When you do what you have done always, you will never reach any further" (Horst Wein)

In 2001, I was very fortunate to come across the work of Horst Wein. The Arsenal manager, Arsène Wenger, had advocated the German expert's teaching methods for the development of younger players during an interview in *FourFourTwo* magazine and I was keen to learn more about his work.

At the time, I was looking for a new approach to coach younger players at the 1v1 Soccer Academy. I had left the provincial program (coaching at the U14/15 level) and wanted to ensure that the development methodology that we used would be successful in developing skilled and intelligent soccer players at the younger age levels. As luck would have it, Wein came to Canada that spring and I was able to attend his coaching clinic and write an article for Inside Soccer magazine about his methodology. (The full article is on the *www.soccer-coaches.com* website.)

What I liked most about Horst's methods was that they were built around kids, and how they learn naturally. In his work he uses many proven techniques used to teach kids school subjects such as mathematics and languages. In Horst's development model the difficulty and complexity of simplified small-sided game activities are increased over time to match the natural physical and intellectual development of the players. Kids thrive on competition and on playing tag games after all (it is what they do from a very young age) and we know that, until their teen years at least, they have the inability to concentrate for long periods at once. They get bored from time to time! So why not provide them with variety (something new every 15 minutes) and incorporate competitions and multi-lateral games (the fancy name for tag) into their training to improve co-ordination?

These are not necessarily new ideas at the youth level. However, what separates Horst's model from others is the different roles of the coach and the players.

Of course Wein's methods are complex, and he has filled several books and lectures in explaining them. But they can be summed up briefly as follows

- Take a more holistic approach, incorporating training and learning that will enhance all aspect of a young player's life — not just soccer skills.
- Develop co-ordination, leadership and tactical awareness in addition to just technique
- Train via a logical progression of development based on intellectual and physical capabilities of players
- Follow a "menu" of activities during one session, changing activities every 15 minutes

- Build bridges between learning a subject and correctly applying it. Within this approach, training and competition are considered one unit, and not two distinct developmental aspects.
- Focus on how skill should be best applied: when, where and why.

Within Wein's methodology, the coach:

- Places the player as at the centre of learning environment.
- Uses questioning to prompt players. He or she guides them to "self-discover" the best way
- Assigns players roles and responsibilities to develop leadership
- Uses "nature". Understands and allows kids to take breaks and come back to soccer learning when they are refreshed (play on swings or go swimming).

And here is how Wein views the role of the player:

- They are the main participant in learning process. They receive, process and give information to the coach and fellow players.
- They're challenged to think through soccer-specific problems and discover solutions
- They are encouraged to take initiative and demonstrate leadership (i.e. set up drills)

That clinic I attended with Wein changed the way I approached coaching. I began to facilitate rather than instruct. I started creating situations where the players were allowed to solve their own soccer problems by thinking through the best way to succeed and trying different solutions until they discovered the correct approach. My players were given more responsibility to set up their own activity stations in order to teach leadership and responsibility.

In Ontario at the moment of writing (2013) we are in the process of implementing Long-Term Player Development Model (LTPD) which is a philosophy for young players to play small-sided games at the younger ages and take away the competetive element of scores and league standings. These ideas were central to Horst Wein's work over 10 years ago. I remember a very important comment that he made at the coaching clinic I attened

"Even if young players want to play 11v11 at an early age, then why are we letting them?....You wouldn't give a 10 year old the keys to your car, they are not ready."

Horst Wein is a pioneer with respect to youth development. Considered a coach for the world's best coaches, Horst Wein has consulted for top clubs such as FC Barcelona, Arsenal, Inter Milan, Sunderland, Leeds United, Atletico Bilbao, Villareal, Real Sociedad, Bayer Leverkusen, VFB Stuttgart and Schalke 04. He has also worked with the National Federations of England, Scotland, Spain, Italy, Austria, Germany, Russia, Estonia, Sweden, Denmark, Finland, Argentina, Mexico, Uruguay, Colombia, Chile, Peru, Ecuador and Venezuela. One of his football books, Developing Youth Football Players, became the official textbook of The Spanish Football Federation — the home federation of the 2008 and 2012 European Champions and the 2010 World Cup Winners — and The Football Federation of Australia.

The bottom line regarding my experience with people like Horst Wein who stress motivation and innovation above all else is this: As coaches, parents and in fact anyone involved with this game we love, we need to seek out people like this who challenge the traditional methods of coaching. Learn about their work, try it on the training field and observe the results.

Keep pushing the boundaries in your coaching and challenge both yourself and your players in training. That will ensure that you are staying on top of your game and your players will become better.

Lessons from a small soccer nation

Uruguay has a population of just over 3 million. Their men's team is ranked number 7th in world football at the time of writing (October 2013). In 2010, Brazil had more footballers than the entire male population of Uruguay, yet it is the smaller nation who are the reigning South American champions, having won the 2011 Copa America (the tournament to determine South America's best national team). And at the last World Cup (2010), Uruguay reached the World Cup semi-finals. This tiny nation has produced world class players such as Luis Suarez, Diego Forlan and Edinson Cavani. And at the start of 2013, their FIFA world ranking of number-16 put them higher than former World Cup-winners France and Brazil.

By comparison, Canada has a population of 30 million people — about 10 times bigger than Uruguay's —with approximately 800,000 registered players. The US has a population of approximately 250 million people, and more than 24 million registered players. But at the time of writing, Canada ranks 106th in world football and the US is at number 13.

So here's the obvious question: why can a small nation such as Uruguay produce so many great players and enjoy such success with their international teams, when much bigger countries struggle by comparison?

Part of it has to do with the South American nation's rich soccer history. They won the first World Cup in 1930 as hosts, defeating Argentina 4–2 in the final, and won their second title in 1950. There is throughout the country a deep-rooted passion for the game. Their top players also talk openly about the famous fighting spirit of the players from Uruguay. Diego Forlan famously credited the Copa America win down to this:

"We won the Copa America because we have three balls, not two."

Much of their recent success can also be put down to an improved youth development structure that has been implemented since Oscar Tabarez returned to coach the national team in 2006, after a 16-year break in which he coached pro teams across South America and it Italy. Considering re-taking the role in 2006, Tabarez said he would only return to coach the national team if he was also provided with full control over the country's youth development programs. Wisely, the Uruguayan federation agreed!

Based on Tabarez's recommendation, about 60,000 young players aged 5-12 play "baby-football" (5-a -side) with a strong emphasis placed on developing technique. At 12, the better players are then signed by professional club academies. The next steps for these players are to be scouted for their national team program at the U15, U17 and U20 levels. It is from these programs that the top players will aspire to play overseas in Europe's top leagues. Sebastian Coates, for example, was signed by Liverpool in 2011 after starring in the U20 national team.

Tabarez, in addition to improving the technical training at the younger levels has made significant changes within the national team programs. All the age-group national teams work more closely together than before and share common playing systems and values. All the national teams train regularly throughout the year (3 times/week) which is possible due to the increased emphasis on keeping their young talent at home until they are more mature and able to cope with the demands of moving overseas. All the Uruguayan professional clubs work closely with the national programs and understand that training and playing with a professional club academy and gaining valuable international experience playing in the national teams provides young players with the best soccer education.

So what can we, as youth coaches, learn from small countries like Uruguay, who regularly out-perform larger nations with greater resources? Here's a short list:

- Youth development starts with small-sided games and an emphasis on technique
- We need to constantly foster a passion for the game with our young players
- Coaches need to work closer together across multiple age-groups
- Young players require progressive and age-appropriate player pathways that are defined so they can see the next steps forward
- Young players can stay locally longer if they can enjoy top quality training — moving away too early can impact development.

It remains to be seen whether or not less-successful — and bigger — nations like Canada will adapt the Uruguayan model as a path to success. But it seems clear that for any country to build a strong national team program, the Uruguayans can certainly be seen as an example for what is possible for less successful nations such as Canada.

The 1 per cent rule

I know this may sound like an odd comment, but bear with me: Despite all the technology we have available, and a fairly comfortable standard of living that exists for most of us in the West, society today does not help our young people. Pick up a newspaper, turn on the television, scroll through Facebook and Twitter and you will be bombarded with tales of someone blaming someone else for something.

Football (soccer) at the top level is no different. In March 2013, the legendary English side Manchester United were knocked out of the Champions League by Spanish giants Real Madrid. The aggregate score was 3-2 after two games, or 180 minutes of play. United had been leading 1-0 in the second leg after 48 minutes and only had to see the game out to go through. At the 56 minute mark Manchester United's Nani was sent off for what the referee deemed a high and reckless challenge. Real Madrid was able to score two goals at the 66th and 69th minutes to book their place in the next round.

At the game's conclusion, the discussion, debate and fan fury focused on the sending-off incident. Of course, United supporters howled that it was the referee's fault that their side was out of the Champions League. There was little discussion of Manchester United's defending (or lack thereof) for the two goals. Few questioned Sir Alex Ferguson's decision not to start

Wayne Rooney, and then to leave him on the bench until the last 17 minutes.

Similarly, a few years ago, everyone raged at the referee for missing Thierry Henry's handball that led to a French teammate scoring and knocking Ireland out of the 2010 World Cup Qualifying round. It was Roy Keane, Ireland's outspoken former captain, who pointed out that as a manager the focus should have been on why central defenders had allowed the ball to bounce in the penalty box in the first place, and on the poor positioning of his goalkeeper, versus blaming the referee.

So, what does this mean for coaches? Simply put, we need to teach our young players to take responsibility for themselves. They are young, and we know they will make mistakes. In our role, we can encourage and teach them to focus on their own performance levels. That is what they can control. Ranting at referees, blaming teammates, coaches or their parents will not improve anyone's performance; it can only serve to deflect. Ask players repeatedly, during training and at games: What could you have done differently?

A good friend of mine speaks often about the 1 per cent rule. He encourages players to always seek out and execute the little things that would give them an advantage. Maybe it is as simple as getting to training a little bit earlier for some extra warm-up. Maybe it's going to bed 30 minutes earlier. Maybe it's trying new moves in training that you have watched on television. Maybe it's planning ahead so you have a proper snack before training and have hydrated properly. As a result of all these little things, which may in themselves constitute miniscule improvements, players can perform as much as 4 per cent better each week (that's 1 per cent better, times 3 training sessions and 1 game each week). After a month, that could mean being 16 per cent better.

Lots of these little things over a period of time make the difference for young players. They are taking ownership for their development, thinking for themselves and striving to be the best they can be. There is no better feeling in sport, and football is no different, at looking at yourself in the mirror and knowing that you have done everything you could. Coaches and top teams seek out these types of players. Teammates love being around them and parents feel proud knowing that their children have developed a set of skills that will hold them in good stead throughout their journey in life.

Mass media and the examples of many professional athletes won't help much in this area. Instead, parents and coaches must be the catalyst for this behaviour.

When players are young, there are no important games

Two summers ago, I was working with a young player aged 11, in a series of one-on-one coaching sessions. One day, before a session began he approached me and told me that he could not work quite as hard that day. I asked him why. Was he injured or not feeling well? It was nothing like that at all. He said that, in two days, his team had an important league cup game, and he wanted to make sure he was well-rested for it.

I was quite taken back by the comment, but it did make me realize the type of system we have created in North America: One where winning games takes priority over the development of skills. Here I was standing face to face with a young player, whose family had hired me to work with him individually each week, and he was focused more on winning a game two days hence, than becoming a better player.

Back in 2003, when I was Head Coach of a large Ontario youth club I tabled a proposition to the board of directors that all scores and standings should be eliminated from house-league play. I had just returned from the UK after watching academy games played by professional clubs with no scores or league standings kept. I argued, unsuccessfully as it turned out, that if Manchester United and Liverpool did not care about the scores of youth games they played, why should we? The motion was dismissed within minutes and I was told that "the competitive nature of North American society would never accept this."

Thankfully, progress has been made. Ontario is currently implementing a program called Long Term Player Development (LTPD). Long-Term Player Development is a Canadian Soccer Association (CSA) soccer-specific adaptation of the Long-Term Athlete Development model (LTAD) developed by Canadian Sport Centres. LTPD is a scientific model for periodized athlete training and development that respects and utilizes the natural stages of physical, mental, and emotional growth in athletes, and it has already been adopted by major sports organizations in the United Kingdom, Ireland, and Canada. The LTPD program is designed to:

- Promote lifelong enjoyment of physical activity.
- Provide a structured player development pathway.
- Describe best practices for elite player development.
- Create long-term excellence.

In Canada's largest province (Ontario) keeping scores and standings, and promoting and relegating teams involving players under the age of 12, has been eliminated. Old habits die hard, though, and change does take some time. Some parents are still fighting against the change. In the province of Alberta, where youth soccer organizers are considering following Ontario's changes, 60 per cent of adults are opposed to the implementation of Long Term Player Development. The main arguments against are:

- Kids and parents want scores and standings
- Kids need to "learn how to lose"

- We're getting rid of competition and kids need to learn that competition is part of life
- LTPD is just for the "elite" player
- LTPD is only concerned with the recreational player (note that both of these last two points cannot both be true)
- LTPD is being "pushed" by the provincial federations — and a bunch of academics who know nothing about soccer and are trying to tell parents what is good for their own kids.

The elimination of scores and standings will help place the focus back on skills improvements and enjoyment of the game. Yes, all the kids and parents will still know the scores during games and that's only natural. However, we should be doing everything to de-emphasize this. In past years, young players may have played the best game of their lives, lost 2-1 and arrived home devastated by the result. This can only turn young players away from the sport. But to say that "keeping score is a part of life" and therefore is therefore necessary is simply not true in other aspects of kids' day-to-day lives. We don't have "class rankings" in elementary schools, for example, but nobody seems to mind that. There is lots of time later to introduce young players to wins and losses, when they can better understand competition and what it means. By that time they will have developed their skills and fostered a rich passion for the game.

As coaches, we can provide our young players with other measurements of success during games. How many consecutive passes can our team make? How many quality crosses can be made into the penalty area? How many shots on target can we take? How many step-overs can our players perform? Maybe that was a move that we spent time on in training that week — and therefore a great indicator of progress.

Let's be creative and ensure that the kid's game remains a game for the kids. Let's not apply adult structures to their playtime. There are no important games when you are young, just more and more opportunities to enjoy the world's greatest sport.

Don't obsess about the facilities

As a coach, I've always taken the view that we must maximize all our available resources, as best we can, to provide the best learning environment possible. In truth, state-of-the-art facilities didn't play a role in my own development. Growing up in Northern Ireland meant muddy grass fields, ash cinder pitches and school gyms for 5-a-side training. Not much changed when I trained with English professional club Swindon Town in 1985. I trained with the first team during my ten days there which meant climbing at 9:45 am into a small mini-bus and driving around Swindon trying to find an empty patch of grass to train on. Just like when we played at school back in Belfast, more times than not, clothing was used as goalposts. Colin Calderwood was captain of the Swindon Town team back then and later went on to play for legendary English club Tottenham Hotspurs and the Scottish national team. He is currently Norwich City's assistant manager in the English Premier League, and I've often wondered what his thoughts must be now when he sees today's young academy players train at elaborate training complexes.

At 1v1 Soccer FC we have trained on bumpy grass fields, bumpy fields without grass, well-maintained grass fields, state-of-the-art artificial turf fields, small-cramped gyms, large double-gyms with cushioned floors and indoor and outdoor tennis courts. We have recently moved more of our programs (indoors and outdoors) to large turf fields so that we can run multiple classes at one location. This owes more to my own obsession to oversee all the training, rather than a direct shift towards working out of the best facilities.

But what do facilities matter, anyway? Just over two year ago I came across a great quote by Daniel Coyle, author of *The Talent Code*. "Here's a little-appreciated fact about talent hotbeds," writes Coyle. "Their facilities tend to be rundown. Rusty. Makeshift. Overcrowded."

Consciously or not, I had been putting that principle into effect for years. One of my favorite facilities to work at is a run-down tennis club facility for winter futsal training. It is cramped and we typically train more than 24 players using two tennis courts. The surface is perfect for the futsal balls we use and the surroundings suggest to the players that they really have not made the big-time just yet!   We have had many families tell us that our training program and coaching is great but our quality of facilities (and this indoor one in particular) means that they will not be joining our program. I don't disagree with them, but let's just say that their perspective on training facilities gives me a pretty good idea of what their priorities are!

Last year we used this facility (winter) in conjunction with a private school's outdoor field which was bumpy and had only sparse grass. During an 18 month period using these facilities, we took 1 player to Sevilla FC (Spain) for a trial, had 6 players invited to train with Toronto FC academy (MLS) and 16 players were invited to the Wolves FC academy in England. Creating a strong training environment is key and I am a disciple (influenced by Daniel Coyle) of the importance of "struggle" during training. Of course, this may have something to do with my Northern Ireland background!

I do believe that we must attain a certain standard with respect to our training facilities but I do not believe that superior facilities alone develop superior players. If that was the case, Canada — with our many excellent indoor and outdoor grounds — would not have such a poor ranking in the world and Maradona, Ronaldo, Messi would not have developed into some of the game's greatest-ever players. Of course, fantastic players like this do go on to train and compete on beautiful, "pool-table"-like fields. But never underestimate the power of a young player realizing that they've earned the right to play at a superior facility after years of hard work on more basic surroundings.

I like crowded training areas, where players constantly have to "solve problems" to keep their ball under control and in play. This philosophy is consistent with the development of elite athletes in other sports. Daniel Coyle refers to this as the "Power of Crumminess." The German "coach's coach", Horst Wein, also commented recently that "The facilities in England now look wonderful. But remember the Jamaican sprint team has only cones and a field (no track!)." (For more on Wein's innovative methods and ideas, see article on page 58.)

The best facilities are no guarantee for success. In fact they may be an impediment. Journalist Henry Winter wrote an article recently in the Daily Telegraph about Arsenal's latest academy recruit, Jack Wilshire. He sees Wilshire as being a young leader in the mold of some of the English Premiership's greatest players like Roy Keane, Alan Shearer, John Terry and Frank Lampard. In the article, Winter wonders if today's young academy players in England are too pampered, too removed from the old-school, character-forming experiences that separated the successful players from the others — and if somehow, Wilshire has managed to escape the "soft" approach thanks to his innately gritty character. Winter believes the academy system develops neat ball-players but the question remains whether it produces enough players of resilient the character to play at the very highest levels.

So as coaches, let's remember to maximize what you have in terms of facilities. The importance of "earning" the right to play on top-notch fields must not be lost in the path towards excellence!

Answers come from inside and outside the soccer environment

Soccer can be very insular. If you look at the coaching profession in many of the countries in the world where soccer is highly developed, the typical model has been for professional players to retire from their playing careers, be fast-tracked through coaching licenses and then installed as managers of top clubs. In many cases these ex-players have never planned or run a training session, have no experience at leading or managing groups and have lacked the organizational and communication skills to fulfill the role successfully. It was not until 2003 that UEFA began to insist that new managers in the English Premier League had to pass the Pro-Licence course. (At the time of writing it is too early to tell if Toronto FC's experiment in the acceleration of an ex-player into the coaching ranks will be a success. In January, 2013, TFC selected Queen's Park Rangers and New Zealand national team defender Ryan Nelsen to run the team before he had even retired as a player! Let's just say for now that Nelsen's first season did not see his team break its unenviable string of never having earned an MLS playoff spot.)

Simon Kuper and Stefan Szymanski in their excellent book Soccernomics outline the historical insular practices of soccer at the highest levels and the inefficiency of clubs that provide jobs for ex-professionals even when they are not the most suitable candidates. The "new wave" of European mangers like Jose Mourinho, Arsène Wenger and André Villas-Boas has started to change this. Not one of these managers enjoyed successful professional careers, yet they are now recognized as some of the most innovative and successful coaches in the world. Mourinho famously dismissed his lack of success as a player by stating "I don't see the connection. My dentist is the best in the world, and yet he's never had a particularly bad toothache." When asked why failed players often become good coaches he replied that it was because they had "more time to study".

In the North American sporting world coaching is recognized as its own profession, and a successful playing career is not considered a prerequisite for being a high-level coach. Attend a coaching course in the US and you will see many young people, aged 22-26. They will have typically played at the college level or still playing. Contrast that with coaching courses in Europe, for example, which are typically filled with ex-pros aged 36 and beyond. Speak with the young North American coaches, and chances are they will have read books on legendary basketball coaches like Bob Knight and Phil Jackson or football's Vince Lombardi, rather than only books on the top soccer coaches in the world.

Early in my coaching career I read a lot of articles and books by Anson Dorrance, who has one of the most successful coaching records in the history of high-level sport. Under Dorrance's leadership, the University of Carolina has won 21 of the 31 NCAA Women's Soccer Championships and he has developed some of the greatest players in the female game such as Mia Ham.

Dorrance was a head coach at the university level as young as 26 and it was interesting to read that he based many of his training sessions on watching the basketball practices by the University of North Carolina's legendary basketball coach Dean Smith. He discovered that the passing and moving patterns and the principles of transition were very similar for basketball and soccer. He also developed many new and innovative methods of motivating and training young female athletes. He quickly observed that "A man's style of leadership is a very top-to-bottom structure. A women's style is more like a network." Dorrance did stir up some controversy by his assertions that men and women should be coached differently — but he has always stuck by this claim and his results certainly cannot be disputed!

Similarly, Mourinho and Wenger studied sports science and have adapted many training ideas on diet and recovery from other sports to give their teams a competitive edge. Wenger has also studied economics at the graduate level and many observers — including the authors of Soccernomics believe this gives him a huge edge in the transfer market, as he is almost always able to ascertain the correct market value of a player.

When I began taking coaching licenses in Canada, I was required to take NCCP (National Coaching Certification Program) courses which covered the basic theory of coaching all sports, in addition to soccer-specific coaching courses. The great advantage of these courses was that there were coaches from multiple sports in the same room, discussing coaching practices. At one point I fondly remember having to study and explain how I would teach the biomechanics of throwing a baseball. Having grown up in Northern Ireland, I had never thrown a baseball in my life. It was challenging, it took me out of my comfort zone but it was a great learning experience.

Along the same lines of embracing all sports as sources for learning about soccer, the Olympics in the UK last summer seems to have had a positive effect on the soccer coaching community there. It is now becoming less insular. Check out the performance website of the great soccer magazine FourFourTwo (at www.performance.fourfourtwo.com) and you are as likely to be reading a stretching article by Great Britain's three time gymnast Louis Smith, and its adaptability to soccer, as about the secrets of old-school manager Harry Redknapp's coaching success.

I've tried to draw my soccer coaching information from varied sources as well. Nowadays I'm as likely to be reading articles by Daniel Coyle, author of *The Talent Code*, or Horst Wein, who has coached 5 Olympic sports in 53 countries. A quick glimpse at my night table currently shows Malcolm Gladwell's *Outliers* about the culture that surrounds the successful (Gladwell was himself a very successful youth distance runner in Ontario); *Talent is Overrated* by Geoff Colvin; and the *Mind Gym: An Athlete's Guide to Inner Excellence* by Gary Mack and David Casstevens. I always seem to have 2-3 books on the go at once.

As time goes on, we are all starting to realize that it is more important for us to understand how today's generation learns best and apply that to our coaching work, rather than only understanding the technical aspects of the game such as the ins and outs of Barcelona's pressing game. To that broader learning, we can and should be looking at other sports and how other coaches teach.

We can also learn from other areas of endeavor. How do young people learn musical instruments? What strategies do their teachers use to motivate them to practice every day and retain a passion for learning? The journey of a coach involves a path of continuous learning. Look both inside and outside the confines of your own sport for answers on how to achieve excellence. You will find answers in both.

It's True: Soccer players are smarter

Men's Health magazine reported in 2012 that research by Predrag Petrovic (PhD and lead researcher at Karolinska Institute in Stockholm) concluded that soccer players score within the top 2 to 5 per cent of the population when tested on memory, multitasking and creativity. For anyone who has been around our game for any length of time, this (of course!) came as no great surprise.

Soccer is a rapidity changing game with quick movements of the ball, teammates and the opposition. It is a random game when compared to other North American sports such as NFL football or basketball where there are more stoppages and set-plays. Petrovic argues that adapting constantly to a changing environment (which elite soccer players do) develops skills that are easily transferable to executive business functions such as changing strategies and suppressing old, out-dated plans.

We often assume that elite athletes depend upon their physical attributes more than their mental capabilities. However, to play sports at a high level, players face both physical and mental demands. Players require a high level of cognitive skills such as attention, memory and visual processing to read situations and make good decisions. They must also be capable of taking snapshots of information on the field, identifying patterns of play and making decisions on the best way to confront specific opponents.

As coaches, therefore, we should be teaching our young players to multitask, be comfortable with change and to be creative.

Gary Keller, author of a book about enhancing productivity called *The One Thing*, argues that multitasking is neither efficient nor effective and that when we try to do two things at once, we either can't or won't do either well. In soccer, however, players have no option but to combine agile physical movement with the ball with processing information on what space to exploit and how to respond to the efforts of opposing players, in order to keep possession and build attacks against the opposition.

Change within the soccer environment is not restricted to the rapid movements on the field. Young players have to be capable of adapting to changing positions and formations that they play. Their teammates may change from week to week or season to season, and the coaching staff that they work with also typically changes on a frequent basis. One minute they may be playing with a team in form, who are dominating opponents, and the next their team is struggling to keep the ball during games. Many young players also play on several different teams. For example, they can suit up for a club or academy team, a representative team (like district or regional) and a school team — all in the same week!

There is an old saying in soccer that if you stand still, you will be quickly overtaken. As coaches, we must be aware changes that are constantly happening to our young players. Not so we can shelter them from this change, though. Far from it. What we should be doing is teaching youngsters the skills to cope with the changing environments that they face — both on and off the field of play.

So how can we do that? Certain conditions can be set in small-sided games to overload young players and develop multitasking skills. For example, when we introduce multiple balls to an activity then players have to look up, see both balls in play and ensure that they keep the multiple balls apart within passing lanes. Players also have to be careful that their runs off the ball do not impede the passing lanes of the other balls. If you introduce two balls you are essentially challenging the players to play two games simultaneously — and with three balls they are challenged to process information and execute movements while being involved in three games. Remember: if young players can get used to playing this way in training, then when it comes to their actual games, they will find all that "multitasking" much easier.

So, at what age can you ask young players to multi task? I think it can begin very early. 1v1 Soccer has had success with players aged as young as 5 in drills such as attacking towards multiple goals or changing direction and dribbling towards one of four goals that have been placed in the training area. We have even gone step further and provided players with the challenge of dribbling towards the "red" goal or "blue" goal (as we call out the colours) or a goal designated by a number. The young players are thus challenged to process recognition based on colours or numbers and also developing memory skills in remembering which goal to dribble towards.

Creativity in young players can best be developed by constantly challenging them to solve problems for themselves. Frequently we have 10 — 12 players in a tennis-court-sized grid and time how long they can play while keeping the ball within the area. It is often surprising how difficult young players can make this for themselves. First attempts at this can see the ball leave the grid in as little as 5 seconds! However, your players will also surprise you by how quickly they can improve performance and, after a while will creatively retain possession for more than 1 minute!

Of course at that point you should introduce 3 balls. After all, soccer players are smarter than everyone else. They should be able to handle it!

How North American players can play in Europe

As soccer nations, the US and Canada are still very young. With that comes a lack of structure at the professional levels of the game, when compared to the more "mature" soccer nations of Europe.

There are fewer professional playing opportunities for the young North American players and a lack of clear pathways to play professionally. Major League Soccer (MLS) does provide some options for young players; however, with only 19 teams for all of the US and Canada, opportunities are limited. MLS academies typically train 3-4 times/week with one game (which duplicates European academies) but this type of program is typically limited to players within a 1-1.5 hour drive time of the team's training facilities. There is a similar drive-time restriction at various age-groups for young players in England attending professional club academies, but the difference is that there are 92 professional clubs in England, meaning that the majority of young players are within a relatively easy driving time (England is a small country, after all).

During the last three years, we have taken one 14-year-old player to Sevilla FC in Spain for a trial and this spring took 9 young players for a training week at the Wolves FC academy in England. I have been fortunate to observe team players and the academy sessions at both clubs. I would conclude that young North American players have good technical ability and up to ages U12 can more than hold their own. A gap appears from U12-U14, though, on the male side of the game, as the young European players at these ages tend to understand the game better. They take more responsibility during the game for their own performances and those around them. They demand the ball, have a vision for what they want to do, and are more capable of executing moves at a high tempo on a consistent basis. I would say, though, that North American female elite players of any age can, on average, hold their own against Europeans.

By the time they get to the U14 age the young European male players are quicker, stronger and much more physical in their play. On the "development" side of things, they also have sports scientists monitoring their development. In addition they have a clear pathway to a career in professional football and are hungry to succeed. We are still lacking most of these things in North American soccer.

In my opinion, there are a couple of key ingredients young North American players must have if they are to successfully pursue playing options in Europe:

- Accessibility to an EEC passport, through parents or perhaps grandparents, as this makes it easier for European clubs to sign them within European Union regulations
- Commitment to focusing on improving their technicalls skills up to U12 levels
- After U12, be in an environment that mirrors the European model for development — player development over winning (MLS or private-academies)

- Opportunity to train at one of the professional club academies or receive instruction from academy staff of professional clubs (For example, through our affiliation with the Wolves FC academy our young players receive a min. of 6 hours of training from Wolves academy staff in Canada each year with the additional options of being invited to attend a 3 days residential camp or 1 week training at the Wolves FC academy in England)
- Competitive games focussed on improving soccer education versus winning games. Within these games, players should learn what it takes to play multiple positions
- Develop confidence in their ability and mental strength to challenge themselves in training and impose themselves in games
- Opportunities to travel and play in Europe for an extended time i.e. greater than 1 month. These opportunities may also combine education with training as part of an overall development model.
- If our young players are good enough and follow this process then I believe that they can create opportunities for themselves to play overseas.
- It is a very competitive environment in Europe. It is also more difficult for North American players to get signed as they do have to be significantly better than local players. But it is possible and with hard work and dedication, it can be achieved.

Just remember: "Hard work beats talent...especially when talent does not work hard"

The role of parents

There is a funny saying in sports circles about the success of a young athlete: "He or she chose his parents wisely."

But in all seriousness, parents play a significant role in a young player's development. Based on my experiences in the game, this development has a much higher chance for success when parents and the coach have the same philosophy, while at the same time being able to separate their duties.

The coach should take responsibility for technical instruction, teaching the game and preparing the player for the next stages of their development. The parent should be supportive of their child, there to listen and be a confidant. Parents must be the ones to help ensure the emotional well-being of the child and work with the coach to ensure that that the young player retains their passion and enjoyment of the game.

The most important role a parent can play is to take the pressure and expectations away from the child. Let the players determine their own goals, ensure they have a balanced lifestyle and take away the weight of expectations that I frequently see being placed on young shoulders. Focus on the development aspects, as parents and spot-check every so often with the coach to ensure that your child is still in love with the game.

I have experienced a parent talking to their son via video-conference after every training session (while on a trial with a professional team in Europe) and providing non-qualified advice on performance. I have listened as parents use the word "we" to communicate the next step in their child's career in the game. I have experienced parents communicating with players during training sessions and games — contradicting the advice being provided by coaching staff, and generally confusing their child.

My advice to parents is to take a step back.

Help provide opportunities for your child by finding them the best teacher available. Remember what legendary Arsenal manager Arsène Wenger has said: If your child showed passion for playing the piano, you, as a parent would try to find the best teacher available so that they would learn the correct skills. Approach soccer development like that. Also, understand why the child wants to play the game. Is it because they enjoy the social aspect of playing with friends? Do they want to play to be active and healthy? Do they have a deep passion for the game and have a ball at their feet every second? Are they trying multiple activities to find the right fit for them?

All these are good reasons to play and it is important that parents understand this, from the child's perspective. Understand the driving force and you can help the child achieve a good level of enjoyment from the sport. Make sure the child is happy in life and that football (soccer) remains a game — something to look forward to, whether it's practicing or playing a game.

Our young players live in a society where they often can't go outside and play freely. Their "play" is controlled by adults in structured and in some cases sterile environments. Enjoy watching them play with a smile on their faces and enjoy the best gift for any parent anywhere in the world — a healthy and happy child. You as a parent are in pole position to help provide this and you also have the opportunity for the biggest joy.

As a young child, aged 6, I remember vividly setting skittles (our UK version of bowling pins) down in our front living room and trying to dribble a soccer ball through them to improve my ball skills. I remember asking my Dad if he would teach me the next day (Saturday morning) to be better. He did by showing me how to take more touches and keep the ball closer to my feet for better control. My dad also supported me every step of the way as a young player offering advice (he had played in England with professional club Port Vale). I never felt any pressure from him or any expectations. I only felt support and somewhere to go if I needed advice. My Dad is 70 now, I'm 49, and his role is still as important as it was back when I needed help with my dribbling skills.

Parents, don't miss out on that opportunity to share a love of the game with your child. Help give them the gift of enjoying the greatest game in the world for the rest of their lives.

10 suggestions for parents

1. Listen! Let your child tell you about their soccer experiences

2. Find a program that provides them with the best soccer education

3. If they just want to play and not train, let them

4. Spot-check with your child once in a while to make sure they are still in love with the game

5. Work with the coach to make sure your child is enjoying the sport

6. Let them fall down, get up and enjoy the feeling of successfully overcoming adversity

7. Don't tie their laces for them, pack their soccer bag, prepare their water bottle — teach them to do that

8. If you can't drop your child off knowing that they will be in a positive, learning environment, you are dropping them off at the wrong program

9. Have them push you so they can play at the next level. Don't worry what potential programs they're missing, good players always get noticed and end up where they should be

10. Be a parent. Not an agent or coach.

What defines
the diamonds?

It is a hot topic in many soccer circles: What attributes do coaches look for in identifying good players? All of us do have differing opinions but there are several common attributes that coaches at the higher levels are looking for.

Many people would assume that physical attributes like speed and technical ability would be at the top of any list. But contrary to popular belief, attitude and the ability to learn are key factors. If you do have the correct attitude and the ability and willingness to learn it does not matter how talented you are. You simply will not be capable of playing at the higher levels of the game.

I have watched academy training sessions at professional clubs in Europe where the most talented players technically have not followed the assigned warm-up, only played at the level they are capable of in small bursts and moaned at teammates around them. It is these players that are quickly passed over. The manager and coaching staff, after all, are looking for players they can count on, game in and game out, over a long stretch of time and not just in bursts. I read an interview recently in FourFourTwo magazine with Liam Brady, who for a long time has masterminded Arsenal's youth-development system. He admitted that Jermaine Pennant —

who has had an inconsistent, checkered career at best as a pro
— was in fact the most talented player to come through the
famed Arsenal youth program, but never had the discipline to
make it with this legendary club.

For coaches, it can be the most frustrating aspect of your
work to feel that you have not helped players play to their full
potential. You inevitably try several different strategies before
realizing that some players — and as I have mentioned, their
families — don't help themselves. You can only really help the
players who want to learn. They have to be open to taking
new information on board, trying new things in training and
then trying to apply these in game situations. Coaches should
ensure that they understand what motivates young players to
play, and try to understand how players learn. For example, do
they process verbal or visual cues more effectively? Understand
what motivates them and try things to accelerate their learning.

Talk to many professional players and they will tell you that
their path to play at the highest levels of the game was paved
with obstacles, in the form of many players who were judged
at some point to be more talented than they were. Many of
these players eventually fell by the wayside. They stopped
learning and the others around them elevated their level of
play to move above them.

I firmly believe that the players who have a true love
of the game have a greater chance to play it at the highest
levels. Training is, after all, hard work! There will be inevitable
set-backs along the way such as injury, loss of form or
being rejected. Players like Rickie Lambert of the English
Premiership side Southampton, who just began to make his
mark during the 2012-13 season at the age of 31, spend the
majority of their careers in the lower leagues. At one point in
his career, Lambert had to support his lower-league income by
working in a canning factory. But he kept going, always kept

believing in himself, and he's been rewarded. In summer of 2013, Lambert was even called up to the England team — and scored within seconds of making his debut as a sub against Scotland! It is very likely that he has a strong support system of family and friends around him as well.

Players like Lambert have had to work very hard to get where they are and have a good work ethic to keep learning and stay at the top of their game. At 31, he now plays for England, while some are now doubting how long Wayne Rooney, at 27, can remain at the top level of the game. Who would have guessed that a few short years ago?

One partner club academy Wolves FC defines 5 main attributes that they look for in young players. To be a successful player at Wolves, players are required to have the following qualities:

- Take responsibility for your own attitude at all times. Ensure you set high standards both on and off the field of play.
- Ability to handle the ball under pressure. To prepare to play at the very highest level — a high level of proficiency will be required in this area.
- Ability to learn. The Academy represents a school of football, on this basis, you must be able to take on board information and apply it in training and in games.
- Players must have their own vision of the game. The very best players see "pictures" before anybody else. You will have to display a certain level of game intelligence.
- Whether you are attacking or defending, winning or losing, playing well or poorly, regardless of opposition or playing surface, in wind, rain, sleet or snow, you must have a desire to play the game

Some of these may surprise you, because they don't focus too much on the actual physical aspects of play. But regardless of a player's level, good coaches look at what he or she can become, rather than the players they are today.

Let's educate our young players in the types of attributes clubs such as Wolves FC look for, and help develop them in the work that we do with young players. If our youngsters can develop these types of attributes they will get identified and noticed for higher levels of play!

Overtraining — How much is too much?

I frequently get asked how much training young players should do, and how much training is too much. It is my belief that this depends on the athlete — and also the type of training they are following.

I'm a firm advocate of the 10,000-hour training rule — the theory, as advocated by Malcolm Gladwell and others, that if you truly want to be good at something, you have to devote at least 10,000 to practicing it. That means that if young players wish to become world-class at their chosen sport, they should be training anywhere from 10-20 hours each week.

Of course, the type of training a player follows is also crucial. In soccer, for example, I believe that young players can train for more than the 10-20 hour/week range, without negative side-effects, if the training is based on technique and players are enjoying playing small-sided games. They also have to be in an environment where there is no expectation on winning and losing. At professional clubs in Europe young players typically start training in academy teams at U9 (aged 8). They may have had two years of "informal training" once or twice a week until then, before entering a more structured environment at the U9 level.

At the U9 levels young players in Europe typically train 4-6 hours/week in a team session and 1-2 hours in individual technical sessions. At the U9-U12 levels, training time can increase to 8 hours/week for team sessions and 2 hours in technical sessions. Changes to the academy system in the UK have increased coaching contact time from U9 to U12 from 4 hours/week to 8 hrs/week. For the U12 to U16 age-groups the coaching contact time has been increased from 12 hrs/week to 16 hrs, mainly by having the young players attend the academy 1 full day/week instead of attending school. At the U17 to U21 levels the players are typically training 16 hours/week.

By contrast, let's consider what happens in other sports. Young athletes in the British national cycling program train 10 hours/week at ages 12-16 which increases up to 40 hours/week between the ages of 17-21. Elite British swimmers typically train 15 hours/week from ages 12-16 and 25 hours/week from ages 17-21. Between ages 12-16 young performers at the Royal Ballet School train 25 hours/week from ages 12-16 and 17-21. Even though the physical demands of these activities are different than those placed on young soccer players, it is still clear that in terms of the sheer commitment in time, these other sports ask a lot more of their participants when young.

In North America, young soccer players typically start playing as young as U3 and can be involved in club academy programs by age7 or 8 and training 2-3 times/week by then. In my opinion, it is not the volume of training hours that places physical and psychological stress on these young players but the quality of the work. Having young players work on their technical ball skills with futsal-type training where they are training the majority of their time individually with the ball or within small groups, allows young players to develop at their own pace without the pressure of winning games. They can take responsibility for their own development in these types of environment, experimenting with new things.

At European academies there is no real focus on physical development until the age of 14. This contrasts with the environment in North America, where the pressure on coaches to win games in order to qualify for the highest-level leagues, means that development becomes short-term. Coaches in this environment tend to believe that they can improve team results through a greater emphasis on fitness and other physical attributes. As a result, a greater physical demand is placed on young bodies that are still growing and developing.

Another significant difference from elite player development in Europe versus North America is that in Europe, programs typically run 42 weeks. That's right — and it can be hard for North Americans to believe — there are 10 weeks during the year when players get to take a break. Youngster are given significant time off at Christmas, Easter and also during the summer months. In North America, players typically do not take time off during the course of the year, other than perhaps a quick few days at the end of the summer competitive season. All elite athletes should have significant down-time during the course of their 12 month training cycle in order to recharge mentally and physically.

Here's another factor we need to keep in mind when thinking about over-training that is often overlooked, but makes so much sense it's amazing we don't do it more often — we need to check with the players themselves about how they feel their training load is affecting them. When parents ask me whether their children are over-doing it, I typically ask that the athlete keep a log on their physical energy levels and mental state (mood) after each activity. This allows athletes and their families to fully understand which activities, club team, academy team, school or other sports are placing the greatest demands on the athlete, especially those athletes who play multiple sports. If the athlete is physically or emotionally overwhelmed, then it is time to either cut back on some activities or alternatively work with their coaches to block off "rest days." The athlete will know their body and mental state better than anyone else so I always recommend that they are central to the decision-making process.

Remember — our bodies are quick to tell us when we are doing too much. We have to listen to them — and when working with young athletes, we must help to make this "listening" process clear.

If it's not working...
Change it!

Soccer development tends to go in cycles and always keeps moving forward. Leading soccer countries like Brazil, Holland, Italy, France, Spain and Germany have all at some point been leaders at developing the sport's greatest   talents. We have all marvelled at the great Barcelona and Spanish national sides during the last few years and openly wondered if we would ever see any better teams internationally in the UEFA Champions League and World Cup. But just as it seemed that Barcelona and Spain were invincible, Bayern Munich easily defeated the Spanish Giants 7-0 in the two-game semi-finals of this year's Champions League (May, 2013) and their fellow countrymen Borussa Dortmund defeated Barca's Spanish rivals Real Madrid to set up an all-German   Champions League final, ultimately won by Bayern in a thrilling 2-1 game. Many are now favouring Germany as favourites for the 2014 World Cup in Brazil, even though they are still ranked third, behind Spain and Argentina in the FIFA world rankings.

So how did Germany get good so all of a sudden? As I have always said, player development is a long-term process. The seeds for Germany's current success were planted a far back as 1998, when   Germany suffered a humiliating 3-0 defeat to Croatia in the quarterfinals of that year's World Cup in France.

The Germans had been a strong team in the 1970s, having won the 1974 World Cup, but by the late-90s, they were not content with the level of young players that they were developing for their national teams and began investing heavily in their youth development programs. The national association required that all German Bundesliga clubs (there are 36 clubs in two divisions) had to invest in and operate centrally-regulated youth academies, which were based on achieving certain development standards. As part of this strategy, there was also a financial requirement put in place to spend money earned by a club's first team back into academy development.

These academies have been a key factor in the production of players for Germany's national teams in recent years. In addition, beginning in 2002, about 22,000 girls and boys aged 11-17 started to receive special training under the supervision of some 1,200 skills coaches, at 390 training base camps distributed throughout the country. Twenty-nine full-time co-ordinators were hired to oversee and manage the project which will costs the German Football Association (DFB) approximately 10 million each year.

A real focus for the program has been to find the most talented players at the U12 and U13 age-groups and to provide them with the best possible training and coaching. Players between the ages of 9-12 are considered to be at the optimal stage of their learning process (the "golden age of learning") and quickly absorb and use new information. In Germany, there are approximately 300,000 children in that age bracket. Out of that number, some 10,000 will turn out to be highly talented and will then receive special focus for enhanced development.

Another key component of the program has been the desire to reach as many children as possible geographically. Training is offered at those 390 bases which are distributing as evenly as possible across the country. The objective is for every young footballer to be given the same opportunities to be discovered and receive special training — no matter where he or she lives.

Some people have argued that the same development system could not work in North America, because of the sheer size of our continent and our population, which supposedly would make it impossible to achieve the successes of a smaller nation like Germany.

However, there are many philosophical lessons that we can implement from the German example at all levels of youth development in North America.

If it's not working — fix it!

It is important as coaches that we are assessing the level of players that we are developing. Do they have the key skills to succeed in the modern game? The number of players that your program passes on to higher levels of the game should be a key metric in assessing your program. If you are not developing better and better players, and more and more of them, it is time for a critical rethink. Once you decide on the improvements you need to make to do this, implement them. Even if you are developing talented players on a consistent basis, ask how can you improve the program further. Remember, in 1998, Germany were not happy as World Cup quarter-finalists, and knew they could do better.

Be more inclusive at younger ages

In North America we tend to select our best players very young — around the U10 level — and focus on a limited number of players. There is no guarantee that our most skilled players at U10 will be always be our most skilled players, or even will be the following year. Expose a bigger player pool to the same level of quality training and let them develop all at their own pace. This provides more players with the opportunity to develop.

Emphasize skills development

As I have said above, the time between ages 9-12 is considered the golden age of learning. It is here that we should spend time on developing technical skills. Players can learn how to win games when they get older. At that point, they will have good technical skills and the confidence to play with their heads up.

Consistent Methodology

Player development is long-term. Follow a consistent methodology and players will develop quicker. Layer on more demands as they progress year to year, rather than constantly change the philosophy of information you provide.

Coaching Development hand in hand
with player development

This is often overlooked in player development programs or considered as a separate program. Once you have outlined the philosophy and designed the program, let good coaches run with the program and mentor them alongside the players. Establish a learning environment where players and coaches work alongside each other pushing the boundaries forward together.

Observing the path to success taken by a top nation like Germany is very instructive. It is up to us as soccer educators to look at these kinds of patterns, and adapt them in ways that make sense for our own programs.

One-position players? Forget it!

One of the challenges we face in North America is our tendency to place young players in specific positions at young ages. Typically coaches will place children in positions based on physical size, level of aggression, speed and technical ability. Less skilled players are asked to play as defenders, aggressive players are asked to play midfield and fast and skillful players are selected as forwards. The problem with this is that coaches are typically making these decisions to win games, not to develop players. Rarely do youth coaches allow young players to change positions, and parents and the players themselves start to believe that they can only play, or are best suited to, a certain position only.

This can often lead to tension between coaches and players/parents, as a coach's decision to put a player in a certain position. How many times have coached heard this one: "Why am I being forced to play out of my true position?"

My own personal experience shows that this approach has many flaws. As a young player I played every outfield position. This helped me to gain a good understanding of the game and an opportunity to practice many diverse skills. One week, I was able to try 1v1 moves against defenders and supply crosses for the forwards. The next week, I was playing central defense and using my defensive skills. On our team, we all had preferred positions but we never for one moment limited our thinking to only one specific spot on the field. We just wanted to play and quickly worked it out that the more willing we were to play in different positions the more likelihood that we would get on the field.

This was in the days (yes, I'm now showing my age here!) when there was only one substitution allowed per game and once you were off the field you were finished your game. If you could slide easily into another position there was a good chance of you staying on the field when the coach made that inevitable substitution. I even went a step further and worked it out that we had few natural left-footed players on our team. Therefore, I started working every day on improving my left foot. Through practice I improved to the point that I started getting selected for left-sided positions on the field and ended up playing a large part of my career there, even though I'm naturally right footed.

In today's game players can find themselves playing in more than one position each game as the team may transition through several different formations during a game. Sometimes a team may be chasing a game and play with more forwards on the field or alternatively be trying to protect a lead and play with more defensive organization. With all that going on, players need to be able to adapt and play in different positions. Also, many of today's professional players started their careers in different positions. Lionel Messi, for example, was considered a wide player at Barcelona during his early years and considered too small to play centrally as a forward — and we have all seen since then what he can do in the middle. Cristiano Ronaldo currently plays on the left side for Real Madrid after playing the majority of his games for Manchester United on the right side — and again, we've seen how effective that switch has been.

One of our biggest challenges in North America is to get younger players to embrace the opportunities to play as defenders. They all think they are being "punished" and that is where we hide our less skilled players. (I'm not sure, but maybe this is something that's commonly done in hockey, and has been transported over to soccer in North America?) Recently, we played one our fastest and most skilled players at right back. At the beginning he was quite upset about it. However, after dominating one game when he spent the entire time marauding down the wing and being our main source of attack, he quickly realized the benefits. He was able to see all the play in front of him and arrive late in the opposition's half unmarked. Watch any game at the top level and you will see fullbacks like Sagna (Arsenal), Cole (Chelsea), Evra (Man Utd), Alves (Barcelona) and Walker (Spurs) spend more time in the opposition half attacking than in their own half defending. Good job too because he players that I mentioned are better at attacking than defending!

When I travelled to the English Club Crewe Alexandra more than 10 years ago I was delighted to learn that their academy teams systematically rotated their young players through a different position each playing period. Academy games are typically broken into three periods so coaches can use the games as learning experiences, with one additional break to talk to players and re-set positions. At Crewe Alexandra if a young player started as a left fullback for the 1st period they would play central midfield for the 2nd period and then rotated to play as a left winger for the final period. After every three or four games they would have experienced playing in all positions. By contrast young North American players would typically play two or three seasons or even more playing in only one or two positions. In my opinion this places young North American players at a significant disadvantage. They do not learn all aspects of the game, nor are they exposed to the opportunities to solve different problems on the field. It can also limit their opportunities later on to join higher-level teams, as coaches may have established players in "their" positions.

When I coached the U15 Ontario provincial women's team to the National Championship in 2000, the team was captained by a young player who had successfully transitioned from a striker to a right fullback. She had played striker for as long as she could remember but I had several quality players in that position. She had many qualities that I admired and it was a case of finding a position for her in the team. She embraced the change and went on to captain her province to a national championship and secure a soccer scholarship to a college in the US.

There are loads of examples like this, but the bottom line is that developing young players to play lots of different positions has many benefits — all of which will help players learn the game and progress to higher levels.

The lob of my life

Parents and players in North America seem to use "playing up" — that is, moving a player to compete in an age division higher than their own — as a key measurement of success. On many occasions I have been asked by parents to play their children "up" or let them train "with the big kids." At 1v1 Soccer, we tend to train players of different ages in technical sessions when the majority of work is based around 1 ball per player. However, during team training sessions it is important that players are capable of processing information quickly enough, and understanding the game enough in order to train with players beyond their own age group.

I am a big believer in playing young players up at the earliest opportunity. However, I will do this only once I am confident that they will succeed there and gain significant playing time opportunities. Similarly I think it is important that young players embrace the opportunity to "play down" an age group in certain situations. Sometimes confidence needs to be repaired and young players need to rediscover this in a less demanding environment.

To illustrate, I recently told the parents at 1v1 Soccer about my own situation when I was a young player aged 13. I had made the move up to a higher level of play in a more competitive league and was 10 minutes into my debut in my new team when it happened. I was playing right back and a diagonal cross came in from the other team. I had to run towards my own goal to deal with the cross but had lots of time to assess the situation and make a decision. Instead I rushed, and decided to play the ball after its first bounce as a volley back to my own goalkeeper. The problem was that my goalkeeper had advanced from his line and I was able to play the "perfect" lob over his head and into the back of my own net. (Hey, it would have been a great goal if it had happened at the other end of the field!)

I never recovered from the error that day, and struggled through the rest of the game and a few more afterwards. The harder I tried the worse my form was. I was not enjoying playing and for the only time in my life, I considered leaving the sport. My confidence was shot.

I decided to go back to play for my former team in a less competitive league. Within a few weeks I regained confidence again. The change had allowed me the opportunity to play with less pressure (all of it, after all, caused by myself) and the regain my enjoyment for the game. I moved back up to the higher level team again, full of confidence and within 12 months I was called up to play for our adult men's team in the amateur league at the age of 14. The drop down a level had taken me out of the line of fire, allowed me to refocus, and had rebuilt my confidence.

I know how important this event was in my own development and often wonder how things would have worked out if I had not had the opportunity to drop down a level. Would I have left the sport or progressed so quickly afterwards? Did the strength of knowing that I worked through a bad run of form and managed to overcome it play a key role in my progress as a player afterwards? I think so.

Fortunately in the academy leagues that we play in (Soccer Academy Alliance of Canada) our players have the option of playing down one age group (2 max per team). We have used this approach in the past to ensure that players can play at their "soccer age" rather than their natural age. This year we will use this opportunity to assist players who may be lacking confidence and who have moved from playing for a club team to our academy league program. Depending upon the player, some can take longer to settle than others. For these players, we will work with them to ensure that they are playing on one of our academy teams — and we hope the correct one — and are full of confidence.

One thing is for certain. There is no better feeling for a young player than walking onto a soccer field full of confidence and being the star player that day. That can be more useful accelerator for development than being able to say that you "play up." I should add here that for many parents or players, being able to say you play in an older age groups seems to be a "status thing." But we have to keep in mind that bragging rights are not important… player development is!

As always it is important to keep the end goals in mind for youth development, rather than focus on the short term successes.

Dario Gradi — an innovator and inspiration for youth development

Dario Gradi and the Crewe Alexandra Football academy have had a great influence on my philosophy of youth development. For several years, 1v1 Soccer enjoyed an informal relationship with the English club and on two occasions I was fortunate to travel to England and study their development methods. In addition, Crewe coaches Ray Walker and Trevor Goodwin visited Canada to work with our young players.

Crewe Alexandra is a small club that has fluctuated between the Championship and Division Two — the second and fourth tier leagues — in England. They have a reputation is as one of English football's most flourishing player development nurseries for young talent. In Dario Gradi's time at the club, Crewe has banked more than £20m in transfer fees for players that they have developed, which includes well-known names such as Nick Powell (Manchester United), Dean Ashton (former West Ham/England), Danny Murphy (former Liverpool/England) and David Platt (former Aston Villa/England).

What struck me about the training at Crewe Alexandra was the obsessive focus on technique. All players there are schooled in developing a good first touch, passing technique and being positive in 1v1 and group attacking situations. Dario Gradi has developed a very distinct coaching philosophy and this is religiously followed and implemented by all the coaching staff at the club. Passing and movement is key and an emphasis is placed on maintaining possession, quick passing patterns on the ground and taking the initiative in attacking play. Graduates from the academy are provided with first team opportunities early and the team always maintains its attacking principles of play, even when they are faced with taller and more aggressive opposition in the lower leagues who use long passing up to tall and physical centre forwards as their main attacking plan.

The academy at the club has placed such an emphasis on their academy that Dario Gradi has juggled his responsibilities as first team manager with coaching the U14 academy team and overseeing the academy operations. Imagine a first-level pro club in North America with a head coach that also guides the U14 team! There was no other club in the country that placed such an emphasis on youth development. One of the coaches at Crewe mentioned that at other clubs, if players were sold for transfer fees, the money was rarely ever seen in terms of coming back into player development. At Crewe, though, things have been different. When players are sold, the proceeds are immediately ploughed into facilities or other areas of academy operations that will help generate the next crop of talented young players.

As Dario has frequently said, and it's a line that I like to repeat often for our own academy, our aim is "to develop better and better players, and more and more of them."

Dario's vision in his 30 years with Crewe Alexandra has always been to name an entire first team — that's starters and subs — made up of home-grown players. That was achieved in May 2013 in their league game against Walsall in their final home game of this season. This is a remarkable achievement and one that many more clubs in England are trying to emulate. There is a growing realisation throughout the professional game that spending transfer fees on players who may only stay at the club for a few seasons represents a poor return on investment. Investing this money in youth academies makes more sense — particularly when young players can be schooled from an early age in the club's values, philosophy, and style of play. These players will also develop strong personal relationships with the other players around them, other people at the club and the club's fans. Barcelona and more recently Borussia Dortmund have proven that this development model can successfully work at the highest levels of the game.

Crewe Alexandra has been doing this for great effect for many years. It is the only club outside English football's top two divisions to be graded a Category Two academy club by the English Premiership and they are rightly proud of the players that they have produced and on the way they play the game. As another indication of their "class," Crewe won the PFA Bobby Moore Fair Play trophy 12 times in 15 years during Gradi's reign as manager. What better place to learn the game than a club committed to investing in their youth, playing attacking football, giving young players early opportunities in the first team and epitomizing the values of fair play?

This has all been achieved when they have had to compete in the same catchment areas as Manchester United and Manchester City. While some families were tempted by the larger status of these clubs, many players and their families valued the soccer education that they would receive at Crewe and the knowledge that young players who performed would have clear pathways into the first team and be given a chance.

In November 2011, Gradi stepped down as manager and is now Director of Football and the academy for the club. The club is now managed by Steve Davis — who had played for Crewe under Gradi from 1983 to 1987. Davis, schooled in the philosophy of Crewe's youth development policy echoes the sentiments of his mentor.

"You have to build and give these boys a chance," says Davis. "Sometimes they take you down. Sometimes they get you promoted. You have to add a bit of experience to the team to help them along the way. But you have to be brave and courageous in playing them."

Business as usual, then, at one of Europe's most successful football talent centres — and a model we can all learn a lot from!

Time and patience are essential ingredients

Let's face it: Soccer at all levels is obsessed with short-term results.

The history of the game has provided us with several different ways to play. Fans have seen Herbert Chapman's Arsenal side of the 1930s (with its classic "W M" Formation), the total football played by Ajax in the 1970s, the Milan pressing game in the late-1980s and now the Barcelona tiki-taka style of play that we have been fortunate to enjoy during the last few years.

But Barca's success especially has been the result of rejecting short-term gains in favour of long-term development. The reality is that the "seeds" for the current Barcelona philosophy and style of play were planted 25 years ago by Johan Cruyff. A recent article by Paul Grech called "Exporting the Barca method" argued that the real secret of Barcelona's recent success has been time. I would have to agree with Grech that for lasting player development success, the hard part is not changing or putting in place a new way of doing things but giving those changes and the system time to mature. An entire club must breath and move in the same way.

As a key part of his research, Drech interviewed Enrigue Duran Diaz, a Barca coach who has spent a decade absorbing the Barcelona philosophy and is currently trying to plant the seed of that distinctive playing style at the South African club Mamelodi Sundown. He argues that for a system like Barcelona's to be copied then everyone involved must believe in it — both in terms of the on-field game, and the core values that surround a club. He also argues that setting up the structure takes time and requires many seasons, which may be contested without success as measured by standings and goals. It is his belief that the Barca model cannot be successful if others are looking to copy it simply to achieve short-term results. It's important to remember that many great current Barca stars — like Messi, Xavi, Iniesta and Puyol, just to name a few — have been with the club since they were kids.

At 1v1 Soccer FC, we are establishing a new philosophy and one that challenges the current norm in Canada for elite soccer development. Our players are encouraged to play across multiple age-groups, play different positions and challenge themselves to get outside their comfort zone to master technical, tactical, physical and psychological strategies that are new to North American players. We know this will take time but we are willing to sacrifice the short-term results in our weekend games to develop better players and people who can go on to achieve their soccer goals and be successful in life.

We demand respect for our staff, the game officials, the opposition and in the way our players interact with each other. The rules and spirit of the game must be upheld and the parents must be appreciated for giving up so much to support their children. We encourage our players to do the best they can be at school, and to be good people away from the field. We want to play attractive football, keep possession as a starting point and take the attacking initiative to our opponents.

We want to encourage our players to take opponents on, try things and to be comfortable with failing. When we lose the ball we want to win it back quickly so we can attack again.

(At Barca, players are challenged to win the ball back within 6 seconds of losing possession!)

We want our players to be comfortable on the ball technically, to be capable of making good decisions on the field, to work together and help each other both on and off the field and to learn at each practice and at each game. We want to allow our players to make mistakes, take responsibility for errors, work on learning from these errors and be open to seeking and taking advice to improve.

As our philosophy is different, we come across many problems every day that hinder our progress and what we are trying to do. Change can be difficult and the short-term and immediate results focus within football (soccer) will always add significant pressure. We understand that! However, through education and patience our players and their families are finding the ability to change their mind-sets for the benefit of the players we train. And we ask that those players and families trust us when we ask them in turn to do things they might find challenging — like playing at an unfamiliar position, or playing in an age group not their own.

The bottom line is that, like Enrique Duran Diaz, I am challenged by focusing only on the things that I have direct responsibility for. The short-term set-backs and frustrations have to be set-aside so that we can successfully continue along our pathway of developing better and better players...and more and more of them.

Time and patience are the essential ingredients along the way!

Give young players some responsibility — and watch them thrive!

An important part of youth development is developing the entire person — not just the soccer player. We expect young people to go onto the field of play and make smart, correct decisions by themselves — so it is vital that we begin to develop these qualities early in their development.

I remember visiting the successful Middlesborough FC youth academy in England a few years ago. On my visit, 'Boro CEO Keith Lamb expressed his puzzlement that "we do everything for the players during the week and then ask them to go out on a Saturday afternoon and think for themselves." That is true of most clubs, at all levels of the sport. The Middlesborough players at the time received weekly and monthly schedules outlining, down to the hour, where they should be and what they would be doing. The club had the players report early in the morning, fed them breakfast, trained them, fed them lunch, trained them again or outlined their gym work or other activities for the day. These players literally had to "follow the bouncing ball," without much of a true opportunity to work out problems for themselves.

Most youth academy programs in Europe are tailored similarly. The clubs wish to monitor diet and rest as much as possible, so they have players eat breakfast and lunch at the club. Players do not have to take much — or any — responsibility for their daily schedule. Many clubs even supervise education and study time at the club.

When I was visiting the Crewe Alexandra academy more than 10 years ago, I noticed that they strived to have their young players take greater responsibility for their development. They had each player rate themselves after every game on a score from 1-3 (Poor/average/good) on the following criteria:

- Preparation for Match/Enthusiasm
- Team Attitude (We not Me)
- Individual Goal One (assigned by coach for each game)
- Individual Goal Two (also assigned by coach for each game)

They also had the young players give themselves a performance score (out of 10) for their overall display, as well as describing their best and worst moment of the match. The players completed this information after every game and handed this (in their player book) into the coaching staff. The coaching staff then provided their own feedback, in terms of scores and handed this back to the players. (Talk about two-way communication!) There was also room in the player book for the coaching staff to assign their own measurement criteria to the players. For example, they may have a central midfield player evaluate their creative passing ability during a particular game.

This kind of performance feedback is critical for elite athletes. They must understand their current performance levels, and must be seeking improvements on a daily basis. They must learn to take responsibility for their performances (during training and games) and must be able to understand their own strengths and areas of improvements. Without this constant feedback loop, young players can go on for long periods of time thinking that they are performing well, when the coaching staff do not agree. Or, they may lack confidence that they are doing well, when in reality the coaching staff are very pleased with their progress. In the end, it really is true that both coaches and players (and indeed, parents) must be on the "same page" (literally at Crewe Alexandra!) regarding how a young player is doing.

This type of feedback program also deflects the importance of team results and highlights the importance of developing the individual player. This is a philosophy that is still developing throughout North America. In a society that is by its nature very competitive, many coaches, parents and players look at only one metric — winning or losing — to measure success.

A former boss once told me that if you wish to improve something, then measure it. It is important that youth coaches decide what the metrics are for their program and to find an easy way to record that information. Involve your players in this process, give them responsibility and then watch them thrive. Think how good they can become when both the coaching staff and the players themselves and their parents are all focused on the same goals, and are both in constant communication about these.

"Navigating" parents:
A challenge and
a blessing

One on my greatest challenges as a coach here in Canada has been to understand the North American parent. I do not mean that with any disrespect. The lack of understanding is more as a result of my own upbringing. Raised in Northern Ireland, I did not begin to play organized games until aged 10. We simply played on the school playground, with our mates in the streets or went outside by ourselves to improve our skills. Many of the activities I work on with players for my personal 1-on-1 sessions were developed when I practiced by myself or with a few friends in Lisburn and Ballynahinch as I grew up.

I think my mum has watched me play in 4 games in almost 40 years of organized soccer — and two of those games have been in the over-40 league that I currently play in here in Ontario! My dad, an accomplished player who played for Port Vale in England, never gave me instructions from the sidelines, even when he coached me in an adult team, when I was 14. We chatted about games afterwards for hours but his comments were always measured and more in the form of advice after I had identified situations in games that I had found challenging.

When I coached the Ontario provincial team, I had little interaction with parents. The team manager typically interacted with moms and dads on administrative issues and the coaching staff and me were left to get on with improving the 13- and 14-year-old players' performance. In 2002 I started dealing directly with parents when I became Technical Director of the Burlington Youth Soccer Club. The club –one of the biggest in Canada — had over 6,000 youth players, and as you can imagine, there were quite a few issues that had to be addressed with parents.

What struck me was how each game became such a catalyst for complaints. Playing time, results, what positions players played in, the formation the team used, the information provided by the coaching staff all became topics for analysis and discussions. Everyone seemed to have an opinion and the latest solutions. On many occasions the players themselves were happy with situations but the adults clearly were clearly not.

I had to try and understand where this behavior came from. Not having witnessed it growing up, I had to try and make sense of it all. I came across a book called Just Let the Kids Play, by the former NBA player and children's sports author Bob Bigelow, which helped provide me with an insight into the competitive sports environment in North America and how adults have taken centre stage in the playtime of children. The increased commercialism of sports in general has certainly contributed to an environment of stress, anxiety, jealously, tension and a fear of failure. Parents are investing longer hours and a greater proportion of their incomes in supporting their children as they play competitive sports. With that investment comes a higher sense of expectations placed upon children and the coaching staff who are there to mentor the young players and make them better. Game results have become the overriding metric in determining if the investment is worth it. Even when game results are positive an emphasis is then placed on how well their child has done, in comparison to the other players.

Here's an example of what I am talking about: In 2000 the Ontario team that I coached had just won the national championship and we had nine players chosen to try out for the national team program. By anyone's reckoning, that is a good outcome! But, within 5 minutes of winning a game against Quebec to capture the national championship, I had the parents of our reserve goalkeeper approach me to tell me that, at age 14, I had ruined their daughter's career by not playing her in the final. (By the way, this player actually later went on to represent Canada at the international level, so I am not sure anything had been "ruined!").

More recently I have had parents approach me with the following concerns:

- Not happy with the position that their child was playing in — "they don't like playing defence."
- Not happy with playing time. Their child had played two-thirds of a game as a U11 player playing up in a U12 team.
- Parent not happy that player was asked to play defense as they "don't know how to play in that position." (Which is exactly why they were asked to play there — to gain knowledge that will come in handy later on!)
- Parent not happy that players were being moved up and down and playing in different positions as the team would play much better and archive better results if there was more "stability"
- The team is not opening up and finding space.

It is difficult to manage this on a daily basis when there are 65 players within an academy program. We have long advocated that our program is based on development of the individual players, and so players will play up and down (within a one year age-bracket) based on what we feel is the best decision for their ongoing development. If we can play players down an age group to increase playing time or improve their confidence, we will continue to do so.

As well, I am a firm believer in players trying different positions to improve their overall game understanding. But even after outlining all these program objectives and regularly communicating them, all this tends to go out the window when young players are placed in a game situation.

Even when scores and league tables are not kept, it seems that players can train well all week, improve skills and enjoy the sport — but in the minds of their parents this all seems to count for nothing if the young players cannot "deliver" during the weekend games. Rather than adopt the patience required for long term development, parents want immediate results, right then and there. And when that happens, either the player themselves gets criticized by the parent, or the surrounding players (teammates) or the coaching staff are found to be at fault. Sadly, I have to say that when I end up hearing parental comments in the aftermath of games, the criticism is almost always levelled at teammates or coaches. Somehow, when a parent is out to find fault with what they have seen in a game, that fault almost never lies with their own child.

But here's a startling fact: An estimated 70 percent of children who play a youth sport end up quitting by the time they are thirteen. That is a very significant statistic and one that all of us as coaches, parents and administrators should, frankly be ashamed of — and one we must work harder on to improve. Many sports are now implementing long term player development programs with initiatives such as no scores and standings being kept. This is a positive step in the right direction. However, until we can place a greater emphasis on the values of teaching and learning at the younger ages and reduce the atmosphere of stress and anxiety that hovers over our young sport games, the players will suffer and we will continue to be meddling in their opportunity to enjoy their youth sport experiences.

Youth games should be viewed as opportunities for young players to showcase their skills and test them against other players. They should play different positions to learn all aspects of the game. They should be encouraged to try new skills during games and praised for attempting to find new solutions to problems on the field. I am writing this today after having coached our U 10 academy team to an 8-nil loss. The players were tremendous and every one of them tried to play against larger and more powerful opponents. When we had the ball they tried to keep possession and be creative, taking the game to our opponents. They played with the same passion in the last minute as they did in the first. They played well and learnt lots. The parents recognized the good technical skills that they have and that they gave their all, and they admired and respected the abilities of the opposing team as well. The opposition coach applauded how our players played and one of the other team's parents did the same. I was proud of each and every one of them and told them so. Tomorrow I will open my emails and will get to review the opinions on the games played by 4 other of our academy teams.

If the players on the other 4 academy teams played to the best of their abilities, enjoyed pitting their skills against opponents and learnt as much as the U10 team then we all can be happy. Either way, the process of development will continue at tomorrow night's training sessions, the night after that and the next session after that. You never stop learning in soccer and that is the truly magical part of the game we all love so much.

Let youngsters play, let them develop and let them enjoy it. They only get to enjoy one childhood ... and it is not ours to take away.

Apply within: Passion and enthusiasm required

Soccer is a passionate game. It captures the hearts and emotion of millions of people throughout the world — in fact, over 700 million of us watched 2010 World Cup Final in South Africa. The players and coaches that I have always been drawn towards are those that radiate a passion and real love of the game. Watch the best players play — like Messi, Ronaldo, Inesta and Xavi — and you get the impression that they could just as easily be at home playing 5-a-sides with their mates. They all have a tremendous passion and enthusiasm for playing.

To help develop this type of player, coaches also have to be enthusiastic and show a real passion for the game. Yes, of course it is important to develop your knowledge of the sport to be able to teach new skills and guide young players through a pathway towards higher levels of the game. However, you must have a true love of the game and also be able to transmit this to your players on a daily basis. This is even more important in North America where youth coaches are typically the focal point of a young player's education. If you live in Europe or South America, you can pop down the street or travel a few hours to watch the games of the world's finest players and learn from watching them. This is rarely possible when you live in North America.

I was fortunate to grow up in Northern Ireland and see great players such as George Best, Kenny Dalglish, and the great Dutch and Juventus teams play in international matches. Top English teams would also visit to play against Irish league teams and on occasions we would travel overnight on the Belfast to Liverpool ferry to watch the top players and teams in the old English first division (now called the English Premier League). In North America young players of today are typically restricted to going to MLS games which, with all due respect, lack the skill levels and passion generated in Europe. That is why we have at 1v1 tried through the years to get to as many of our young players as possible over to Europe to see live games and sample the passion and enthusiasm for the game. They all return much richer for the experience.

So how can you as a coach or parent help fuel passion and enthusiasm for the game?

As a parent you can watch soccer on TV or the Internet from the top leagues in the world with your child. You can pick your own teams and like our family, spend endless discussion and witty bantering debating the merits of each of your teams. You can also play with your child in the park. Some of my best memories as a child were spent playing football with my dad or uncle in the backyard or both of us joining in the mass games (40 a side) that developed outside in the street. (I was especially fortunate to play in one organized game for 45 minutes when I was about 14 with both my dad and uncle). More and more North American families can also travel to watch MLS games as the league is growing in quality and adding more teams.

As a coach it is also important to foster a love of the game. As you may have guessed by now, I'm an avid Arsenal fan, and many of my players have shared my trials and tribulations of going 8 years without a trophy! Of course, all of our players have their own teams and I like to encourage the light-hearted banter before and sometimes during the sessions. I always remind players that Manchester United shirts are banned from all 1v1 Soccer events and the rest barely tolerated!

As well, many Champions League games are now televised in North America, so many of our young players have been able to enjoy the close rivalry in recent years between Barcelona and Real Madrid. They also have their own opinions on whether Messi or Ronaldo is the best player in the world. They buy their heroes' shirts, wear their boots and more importantly try their latest moves. Many players are also big fans of the FIFA computer games. The game has helped teach them strategy, and has introduced them to all the players from the top teams, allowing them to build super teams by assembling the top players in their squads. I must admit that I get excited too about imagining Messi, Ronaldo and Luis Suarez as the three forwards on any team!

Most of the players that I coach do not know of George Best, Pele, Maradona or Johan Cruyff — the legendary players that my generation was brought up with. However, we can share the latest exploits of Messi and Ronaldo. Our coaching staff can also encourage our players to watch certain players and try and copy their skills. Many of our young players live-stream games from all over the world and we can also send out video clips of the world's best players to help teach certain skills.

At the core is a deep passion and love for the game. You must have it be a successful coach in my opinion. You must also foster it and maintain it. When you are deep into scheduling, addressing parent concerns, pumping balls up and lugging equipment across the field, you must remember your deep love of the game. You must then pass that along to the next generation.

It is the greatest gift that you can give as a coach.

Lessons from Sir Alex

Sir Alex Ferguson retired today (May 8, 2013). After 26 years managing Manchester United he has decided to stop coaching at 71 to begin a new adventure in his life. Since announcing his retirement everyone has talked about the number of trophies that he has won during his glittering career. In a management career spanning 39 years he has indeed been extremely successful. In total his teams (Aberdeen in Scotland and Manchester United) have won 48 trophies. There are however many lessons that we as youth coaches can learn from. Here are 10 of the most significant:

1) Dedication and passion for your work

Up until the day he announced his retirement, Sir Alex had never missed a day of training at Manchester United. He was the first one to arrive at training and the last one to leave. At his first club (East Stirlingshire in Scotland, a team that did not have a goalkeeper when he arrived) he was a part time manager and combined his coaching duties with running a bar that he owned. His typical day was spent working at his bar during the daytime and training at night. He left the house at 6am and returned home at 12 midnight. Sir Alex has maintained this level of dedication throughout his career and anyone who has seen him coach from the sidelines will never question the passion he had for his work.

2) Think big in terms of goals

When Sir Alex took over at Aberdeen Football Club in his native Scotland in 1978 the club had not won the league since 1955. He quickly set his sights on breaking the monopoly of Rangers and Celtic in the Scottish game. No team outside these two clubs had won the league for 15 years. It would have seemed an impossible dream but Aberdeen went on to win 10 major trophies in 8 years to become the most successful club in Scotland. In short, he had within 8 years broken the Old Firm (Rangers and Celtic) duopoly. In addition they went on to defeat Real Madrid in the final of the 1983 European Cup Winners final.

When he was appointed manager of Manchester United in 1986 the club had not won the league title since 1967. Liverpool had dominated English football and won the European Cup 4 times since Manchester United's win in 1968. Sir Alex famously set his goals as " knocking Liverpool off their ★★★★ing perch."

3) Don't let your standards drop

Many of the players who have played for Sir Alex have spoken of the high standards he expects from everyone. Players are expected to be fully dedicated and focused on the next goal. They are expected to come to train every day, and on time, with the mentality to learn and become even better. When his teams won championships, they celebrated — but the hard work began the following day as the players prepared themselves for the next challenge.

4) Believe in youth and long term development

It was not all plain sailing for Sir Alex at Old Trafford. His first 4 years at United went by without the team winning a trophy. Many believe if he had not won the FA Cup in

1990 then he would have lost his job. Despite the pressure on him and the short-term nature of the need for results in the professional game, Sir Alex set up the best scouting network and academy program in the country.

He held firm to his belief that the young players he was discovering would eventually play a significant role in the club's history. In 1992 Manchester United won the FA Youth Cup with players such as Ryan Giggs, David Beckham, Paul Scholes and Nicky Butt. In 1999 the club won the European Cup again with all these players in a significant role, and for many years forming the backbone of the team that enjoyed such success.

In the dark days when Sir Alex was under pressure he stuck to his principles and his faith in these young players. On many occasions he would go with his assistant manager Archie Knox to train these young players in cold gyms in Manchester. Others may have focused more on more pressing and immediate first team matters but not Sir Alex. In the current squad Darren Fletcher, Jonny Evans, Tom Cleverley and Danny Welbeck have all been developed in the Manchester United academy to continue this rich legacy. This constant production of home-grown talent has allowed Manchester United to continue to dominate English football.

5) Mentor your young players in life as well as soccer

David Beckham also retired recently (May 19, 2013) and has spoken of Sir Alex being like a father figure to him when he moved from London to Manchester at the young age of14. Similar stories have been told by other players. It is clear that Sir Alex has played a significant and positive role in transitioning many of his young players from young apprentices to seasoned professionals. This is only possible if you understand your players as young people, and are prepared to help them with life issues as well as soccer ones. Developing good young people is by far a more significant achievement than developing good young players. In my opinion they go hand in hand.

6) Adapt to changing times

Sir Alex is well known for the "hair dryer treatment" (yelling and screaming at players from a short distance away), and he especially seemed to favour this approach in his younger days in management. What is clear is that he has adapted with the times. He openly acknowledged that he has had to adapt, as the son of a Glasgow shipbuilder, with players getting pedicures, wearing pony tails and getting massages. If you follow English soccer, you will know that at different times in his career, "Fergie" has had to manage such characters as Carlos Tevez, Wayne Rooney, Beckham, Eric Cantona and Dimitar Berbatov — to name a few — and has gotten the very best out of each of them. It is a very different world than when he entered management. The players are very different and as a coach you have to adapt to the changing times.

If you ask Wayne Rooney if Sir Alex is any easier to please now than he was 10 years ago, he will likely say no. However, the methods have changed to fit the personalities of today's generation. Sir Alex has been smart enough to recognize this and to change accordingly — and so should you as a coach.

7) Delegate

In recent years, as the demands of running a top professional club have increased, Sir Alex has surrounded himself with a top staff of technical coaches and sports scientists. One manager (Neil Warnock, formerly of Leeds, Crystal Palace and Queens Park Rangers, to name a few) told a story about playing Manchester United at Old Trafford. Warnock was watching the horse racing on television with Sir Alex before the game when suddenly he realized that the game was close to beginning and he had not given his team their pre-match team talk yet. Sir Alex by contrast was relaxed and enjoying the racing. The Scotsman knew he had a very competent and dedicated staff in place to prepare the team for the game, even when it was only minutes away.

8) The team is bigger than any individual

David Beckham and Roy Keane are two of Manchester United's biggest stars who learned that their goals had to be in line with those of the team. When Sir Alex felt that the performances and focus of Beckham was being compromised by his activities off the field he was quickly sold to Real Madrid. When Roy Keane, club captain at the time, was critical of his younger teammates in an interview, he was quickly released by the club, despite his previously outstanding service. In your own youth team, decisions should be made in the best interests of the group and not dedicated by individual players, no matter how good they are.

9) Get behind your players in tough times

Sir Alex Ferguson has always defended his players, even in public when very different words may have been spoken in private. Young players will make mistakes, both in soccer and in life. If he had not travelled to France to speak with Eric Cantona after the goal-scoring genius was famously banned for 9 months after attacking a fan, "King Cantona" may have quit the sport and been lost to the game as well as Manchester United. Young players can still learn from an arm around the shoulder when the going is tough. They might just need encouragement when they have made mistakes and your understanding, patience and belief in them can propel them forward as young people.

10) Keep a healthy life balance

As coaches we put in long hours away from our families, working nights and weekends. It is no different for coaches at the very top. Sir Alex has spoken this week about the strong support that he has enjoyed from his family. He also has spoken about taking time away from the job to go the movies with his wife and enjoy his other hobbies such as horse racing, travelling and wine tasting.

This final lesson from Sir Alex is to take time out and find a balance. I've not always practiced what I'm preaching but I am getting better at it and my family deserve it. I'm also a much happier and better person as a result. You may have to delegate more and learn to switch off, but it is very much worth it.

When you coach you have to be all-in

One of my favourite movies is the 2011 hit, *Moneyball*. It is about Billy Beane, general manager of the Oakland Athletics baseball club, and his efforts to successfully compete against the larger Major League clubs such as the New York Yankees with a fraction of the budget. To compete successfully, Beane — played by Brad Pitt in the film — had to reinvent how Oakland selected players, and ran their team. At one point he turned to his trusty assistant, Pete, and says "It's just you and me Pete…. we're all in." (Just as a side note, Beane has an interesting soccer connection, as he is a big admirer of the legendary Arsenal manager, Arsène Wenger, and the two reportedly have met from time to time to discuss their views on player selection.)

When you are trying to change a mentality and introduce new ideas you become an easy target for criticism. I have lived with this for the majority of my coaching career in North America. I understand that what I am trying to do is much different than the typical competitive system and that it is not for everyone. I know the rules and I am prepared to fight for what I believe are the best methods to develop young soccer players in North America .

During a few recent challenges at 1v1 Soccer, I drafted an open letter to our families reemphasizing our philosophy

and how much we were committed to following our beliefs
in developing the best soccer players that we could. I have
included a copy of the correspondence below. As a coach you
have to be, as Beane says, "all in" — and you have to be willing
and able to communicate this to your players and their families.

Dear 1 v1 Families:

As you know, this has been a challenging week for 1
v1 soccer. But as a firm believer in turning challenges
into positive opportunities for long-term development,
I have been thinking a lot about whether our program
is truly set up to develop young soccer players to their
fullest potential. And after a lot of soul-searching, I
have to conclude that our 1 v1 training program and
philosophy truly does bring the best elements of soccer
development from around the world into the best
possible "package" I can think of. That is, after all, why I
believe so strongly in it, and have devoted my life to it!

I think it is useful to consider our program as a triangle.
On one side is the player, and the dedication and
commitment he or she brings to every training session
and game. On another side are the coaches, who bring
technical expertise to competitive and developmental
situations. And on the final side are parents and families,
who support their kids and believe that the training
they are receiving is right for the young people in their
care.

That said, we have had some unfortunate situations
over the past few weeks that have, if you will permit
me one more use of the metaphor, truly "weakened
our triangle." We have had players (and parents) tell me
they are unwilling to move to a younger age group
for SAAC games, and others constantly insisting they

should "play up" in an older group. Others have been unwilling to try to play in field positions they feel are "not theirs." Although I have been stressing both the importance of playing at a level best suited to a player's current developmental level, and the need for players to develop by becoming comfortable as defenders, midfielders and strikers (and occasionally even keepers), I have still been receiving push-back in these areas.

I don't often take a "hard-line" in these matters, but given the thinking I have been doing over the past week, I will in this case. I will admit that in some cases, the "fit" between 1 v 1 and some players and their families might not be the right one — and that our views about developing players will differ. If that is the case, I will not hesitate to bring to an end any relationship between a player, parents and 1 v 1 that does not seem to be in the best interest in a strong "triangle" as I have described above. Soccer is too much fun — and life is far too short — to be spending time in a program that is not meeting the needs of everyone involved, and to be honest, I am far too committed to what we have built at 1 v 1 to change some of our basic cornerstone philosophies to suit the short-term needs of a handful of parents and families.

In the coming weeks, I will be speaking to our families and players more about this, but I wanted you all to hear the basic message from me at this time.

Helping young players to achieve their soccer goals

I always find it important to understand the soccer goals of the young players we work with. It seems obvious, but knowing what a player wants to achieve is the only way we as coaches can help motivate them to get there. At 1v1 we have the players complete a quick self-analysis and ask them to outline both their short and longer-terms goals. As we've often heard, don't start a journey without understanding where you want to end up. So it follows that will need a map for this journey — and that is where our training plans fit in.

Typically, the young players in our academy list playing professionally in the English Premiership or playing in La Liga with Real Madrid or Barcelona as their ultimate soccer goal. And while that's a lofty goal, it's an admirable one. Like any big goal, though, it takes careful preparation to get there. Recently, I came across an article by Lucas Scott that was featured on the Bleacher Report website that outlined his top 10 steps on how to become a professional football (soccer) player.

Scott had at one point been an aspiring young footballer so he is a good source, and he passes along some excellent pointers to young players. It is important for us as coaches to help cultivate some of these traits in our young players as to reach the very highest levels of the game, because talent is not normally enough by itself.

Scott outlines motivation and dedication as being key steps. He suffered many injuries as a young player and felt, looking back, that he had lacked the motivation to overcome these set-backs. His advice was for young players to stick to their goals, even if they had to make sacrifices. We often talk to our young players about the struggles required to become better at soccer and remind them that any set-backs should be viewed as opportunities to recommit to your goals. If you have written your goals down then they can be referenced when the going gets tough. As a coach, you can help young players with this by asking them to focus on the bigger picture and what they are trying to achieve. They will have to dedicate themselves to their goals and ensure that they are doing the right things to achieve them. After all, there's no use aspiring to be a professional footballer in the English Premiership if you are missing training sessions or not performing at your best.

Recently I was training a group of young players, many of whom had listed playing for Real Madrid as their long-term goal. I brought them in for a chat and asked them all what they were prepared to do, over and above what the other players around them were doing. I mentioned that the Real Madrid coach could only pick 2 or 3 attacking midfielders and assuming that there were a few Spanish lads (and others) with designs on those places also, it was important that they were training to their highest ability during our training sessions. In addition, to become the very best, a player should be working on their skills at home also. And youngsters need to be reminded that, as a team game, individual goals need to go hand-in-hand with team aspirations.

Once again, the legendary Barcelona club from Spain provides a great example here. Lionel Messi is not only a very talented footballer but also a great role model for young players. He is very humble and works very hard for his team. After winning the FIFA Club World Cup and being singled out for his individual performances he said, "It's nice to get that recognition of course, but it's something I want to share with my teammates. I couldn't have won an award like this without them." When you show these types of quotes from the world's greatest player to your own players, it can add to your teaching on the importance of being humble and being respectful and grateful to your teammates.

In another article I spoke about the importance for young players to increase their game understanding by playing in different positions. To do this, young players have to be open to new ideas and be willing to adapt. Scott supports this viewpoint in his article by confirming that soccer can be played many different ways. For example, in Italy the game is very tactical and played at a relatively slow pace, while in England it is played quickly and aggressively. Young players must look to learn many aspects of the game and you as a coach must be constantly expanding their knowledge. They must also be developing as young people also and be capable of evolving in those areas also. For example, I always feel that it is important for young players to have the skills sets to successfully cope with change. They may play on real grass one day and on artificial grass the next. They may swap positions during games. They may play and train with different coaches during the same week. They may have to cope with long commutes to training and games and less time to do their homework.

Here's an example of adaptability in action from our own training sessions. I always find it amusing to see what happens when we have an odd number of players and we start to arrange a small-sided training game. Many coaches may play 5 v 5 + neutral player to deal with this. I prefer to play 6 v 5. The players on the short-handed team naturally voice their displeasure at the unfairness of it all. I always tell them to deal with it. Imagine: It's the World Cup final and you have had a player sent off. There are 10 minutes to go and you've no option to get on with it.

Remember: Good coaches help develop good people too, and young people who can cope with what sport and life throws at them. You can have an enormous influence on this. As coaches, ask your players how things are going outside football and what is happening in their lives. They will appreciate that you are taking an interest in them as people too and this will help accelerate their pace of learning.

Creativity and letting players solve problems

When I started 1v1 Soccer in 2000, my main aim — one I haven't changed, by the way — was to provide young players in North America with training and learning experiences similar to leading soccer nations. During that time we have studied training models in the UK, Brazil, Spain, Holland, Germany, and Italy. My main metric has always been how many players we have successfully prepared to move to higher levels of play and the goal remains to have some of our players signed by our partner club, Wolves FC in England or other professional clubs in Europe or North America.

Recently, I came across an article online by Gary Allen, of the Virginia Youth Soccer Association, outlining what he believes is the "stifling" of development for players in North America.

Allen talks about many of the challenges that we have identified as impediments to young players in North America developing to world class levels:

- Fast-tracking players to "play up" age-groups
- Asking players to limit development to playing in specific roles using skills they are already strong at

- Placing players too early in competitive environments where they cannot take risks
- ID decisions being made at young ages to exclude the majority of players

Allen argues that by placing young players in competitive environments too early we are identifying players as young as 8 based on a perceived set of skills based on the "now." The problem with this approach is two-fold. A lot of other players are then excluded from that early age from the best development and coaching opportunities. This is similar to what Malcolm Gladwell outlined in his number-one best seller *Outliers-The Story of Success*. Gladwell argued that in youth sports players born in the early part of the year are typically selected ahead of other players born later in the year due to their earlier maturation of development (for example, the difference between two children, both technically "age 9" but one born in January and one in September, can be huge) and that this separation at an early age means that only a small number (the ones born in January, February or March) received access to the best training programs, with longer hours and the best instructors.

Allen outlines that the second problem with this approach is that if players are selected at age 8 because they are faster and stronger than the other players, then they will be expected to keep developing and using these attributes only, at the expense of developing other parts of their game. When promotion and relegation issues are at stage in youth sports or ensuring that teams are accepted into the top leagues, the individual player's joy and passion for the game soon takes a back (and in many cases a permanent) seat to the overall goals of the team.

I have mentioned elsewhere the opposition many players and parents put up when coaches ask players in North

America to play different positions or consider playing within an age-group which may be a year younger. This can be a problem even when the players are enjoying greater success by improving learning or their overall confidence. It is not "conventional" and therefore not easily embraced. As Allen points out our culture in North America does not allow the "failure" required to learn at any age or stage — immediate success must always be achieved. Remember, the traditional competitive team system in North America has not, as Allen argued, helped produce even one truly world class player in 30 plus years, amongst a population of about 300 million, if you combine the US and Canada.

So what are the solutions? First of all players must be taught the joy and passion of the game. A coach in BC named Rick Gruneau recently sent me an email speaking about some of the differences he had experienced when he spent a week at the Spanish club Espanyol, in 2010. He asked the coaching staff what the two most important things were that they taught in training, the answer was immediate, though, for a North American, surprising: "Joy and technique."

Joy because, as the coaches put it, "We are a small club (compared to Barcelona and Real Madrid) and these players are precious investments for us. Every time a player burns out or leaves the game we not only feel that we have failed the player, we lose our investment in him." And technique, because soccer is "primarily a game where the challenge is to exercise the best technique possible under pressure."

Rick went on to recount his amazement at the "joy" in training sessions when even in the most competitive training there was a lot of laughing and mutual back patting, where players would spontaneously break into applause when another player did something out of the ordinary technically. It was not something he had ever experienced back in Canada.

With joy and passion can come creativity, if we place young players in situations where they are allowed to think for themselves and solve their own problems on the field. This process of guided discovery will help players develop the mindset to take responsibility and think creatively to solve problems. Yesterday I stopped a 4-goal game and asked the two teams to get together and talk about what was happening in the game and how they could possibly make adjustments. They had all the answers and changed things to improve performance. The best comment amongst several good ones was "taking two good touches is better than taking one bad one." It was a very bumpy field so the observation and solution did lead to greater success.

Trust your players and provide them with the opportunities and the time to come up with creative solutions, and you will be paving the way for their future success.

"Success is the prize for those who stand true to their ideas"

We all have our own take on what defines success. The title quote by motivational expert Josh S. Hinds is a favourite one of mine as reminds me of the importance of being true to yourself. When you coach any sport, you will be challenged. You will be challenged by your players, by their parents, by your fellow coaches and if you work for an organization, your employers.

What many don't realize, though, is that the best coaches around challenge themselves the most. They will relive situations in their minds, replay them over and over in their heads and question themselves on a daily basis. Coaching is about leading and facilitating performance improvements. So, it is only natural that the best coaches constantly expect improvements from themselves. The trick is to do your analysis, decide if there was a better decision to be made, learn from that...and then move on.

When I entered coaching, I made myself a promise: I was going to make my own decisions, stand or fall based on what I felt was right and stay true to my principles and what I believed in. I had a vision on how I felt football should be played and have stayed true to several core values. I'm proud to say that

I've kept that promise. Of course, I have made many mistakes in my coaching career but I have never made a decision that I didn't want to make at the time. It is important for me to keep that level of integrity in my work. My wife often teases me that our mortgage would be paid of quicker if that wasn't the case but she says that knowing full well that my approach will never change. It can be a lonely existence because even your closest coaching colleagues do not always agree. However, I have always wanted strong coaches around me as my type of personality requires me to talk things through before I reach important decisions. I listen to those I trust, gather opinion then make my own decisions. If the going gets tough and criticism arrives I stay the course. I made the best decision to the best of my ability at the time.

Standing true to your ideas can be a liability, however, if as a coach you do not continue to learn, evolve your thinking and refine your ideas. If you do not continue to test your ideas with the changing demands of the profession, then the game will pass you by and you will be making misinformed and incorrect decisions. An example would be my own ideas on teaching defending. As a coach I love the idea and the organization required to teach players how to work as a defensive unit. I'm one of those coaches who loves watching attacking football but can marvel at Jose Mourinho and his Inter Milan team going to the Nou Camp a few years ago and preventing Barcelona from scoring. I have run many defending sessions at coaching courses and enjoyed the challenge.

I remember being quite surprised that the legendary developmental coach Dario Gradi did not spend much time at Crewe Alexandra in England in teaching defending. At the time I did not quite understand it. Later I began to appreciate this more when I began teaching younger players as I felt that with limited time it was more important to spend time on basic ball skills, as a priority. In the last few years my thinking has evolved a little more. I think that the art of defending is less important in the modern game. Instead it has been replaced by pressing and forcing opponents into mistakes to win the ball back. Now I do incorporate this type of work in my training sessions. I feel young players should be taught how to close space quickly and work together to win the ball back. The work I do in this area is not like I was taught 15 years ago in my coaching courses! At that time we broke defending down to the finer details of speed of approach, angle of approach, body stance etc. Now, I keep our instructions quite simple. Get close to the ball quickly, and force the player with the ball towards crowded situations where they will be challenged to keep possession.

To the outsider it may seem that my philosophy has changed, given how I have made this switch in how I work on defending. However, in my own mind, I see my role as preparing our players to the best of my ability to succeed within the modern game. If the requirements for the top players are changing then in my opinion the training of our young players needs to adapt also. If we have a clearer understanding that what separates good players from great players is the ability to receive the ball, and then maintain possession and initiate attack even when marked tightly then we need as coaches to spend a greater amount of time developing these skills at the youth levels.

I read a great story about David Moyes recently. Apparently, Moyes, the long-time manager of English club Everton and now boss of Manchester United, had noticed during the 2012-13 season an increasing trend for all the top teams in European to play more through the midfield area. He viewed the midfield as an increasingly important component for teams and realized that managers were using more innovative formations and tactics within this area. The part of the story that I really liked is that he then met with Jim Fleming, head of coaching development at the Scottish football association and suggested some changes to the coaching courses for the next generation of coaches to reflect these changes. This was from a coach who was 10 days away from landing hat arguably one of the largest coaching jobs in the world (managing Manchester United.) I know Jim Fleming from when I took my UEFA B license course in Scotland. He was such a knowledgeable and passionate educator back then and it delights me to know that he like the rest of us he still strives every day to get better.

(Just to add a quick story about Jim Fleming: When I was on the UEFA B License course I mentioned, I pulled my hamstring a few days before my final assessment. I was walking around feeling miserable and worried if I would be able to do demonstrations properly for my final assessment, as for this level of coaching certification, you actually have to do a "demo" to prove you can show the skill or tactic in question to your players — it is not all theory!. Jim quickly pulled me out of this with the famous Scottish gallows humour by saying, "the cross you pulled your hammie wasn't a very good one anyways!" I broke out laughing. He knew the correct thing to say to me right at that moment and it relaxed me. I'm pleased to say that I was able to do well in my final assessment and achieve that license!)

We all have to keep studying the game, evolve our thinking — but at the same time, stay true to our core values. I still want my players to focus on their technical skills and play attacking football with flair. However, I do want them to win the ball back quicker now so we can attack again. I've placed more requirements and responsibility on them. My ideas are the same and I remain true to playing attacking football. However, how we achieve that, and the methods we use in training on how to get there continue to evolve.

I tell my coaches at 1v1 all the time that I coach much differently this year than I did last year and I will coach differently next year. You must keep adding to you knowledge and the methods that you use to deliver your messages. What should not change is staying true to your ideas and how you feel the game should be played. For that you will achieve success. The prize may not come in the form of a big trophy, you may not become richer in a monetary sense, and you may not even get a pat on the back. The prize will be much larger than that — you will know that you are continuing to do the right thing to the best of your ability, and in a way that benefits the people who matter the most: the players!

Youth players:
Not a commodity!

One of the most frustrating things that I continually witness at the youth levels of the game is seeing young players viewed as commodities by coaches, and frankly, even by parents. I've lost track of the number of times I've come across coaches holding back the transfer of player cards or books to new teams or forbidding young players to engage in any form of soccer outside team activities. Many youth coaches have frowned upon their players attending our skill classes, and this year a player has been told by his coach that he can't train for an hour with me on a Monday morning from 8:45 to 9:45 am (in an elite training program at a school) because he has a game at 9 pm on those evenings. And far too often, I've heard parents use the word "we" when talking about a younger player's efforts — such as "we're playing for such-and-such a club this year." That tells me all I need to know about how a parent views their involvement with their child's soccer.

Coaches or teams or event parents do not "own" players. We are there to teach, guide and assist at the youth levels. We are there to provide advice and mentor. We are not there to control, manage and own a player and his or her time. Young players should not be placed in tug-of-war situations between coaches or prevented from participating in outside activities that may help them become a better player or a better person.

Many of our families are shocked when they learn that our academy league does not play on long weekends or that it is ok with us that they take a family vacation in the summer. There are many soccer families that I know who have not taken a summer break for several years as they were told that this would negatively affect the team. There are many very talented athletes who have quit soccer because they are multi-sport athletes and they have been cut by teams who asked them to choose between sports.

Today we came across a situation where two players were prevented from playing for our academy team as trial players because their club coach would not allow it. (There was not a game-day conflict, and we were not asking the players to miss any club commitment.) Not only that but the parent (of one of our other players) who had invited them to play was openly criticized via email for offering the families this opportunity. We were of course criticized for "poaching" even though we have many players in our academy who play for both our academy team and a club team, and in this case, we simply made an inquiry as to whether the players were available.

Lost in all this is the joy that young players are supposed to experience from playing a game. There are more and more situations it seems where the joy of the game is spoiled by adults. Players are not a commodity to be fought over and families should certainly be free to take breaks and have the flexibility and opportunity to participate in other programs. Surely, this decision should lie with the families. We as coaches should simply offer our programs as options.

I've always had the opinion that if a player was not happy to be somewhere, they should not be there. As a coach the last thing that I would want to do is to keep a child in our program against their will or deny any opportunities to young players. I've always enjoyed playing my football and want other young players to experience what I'm still fortunate to experience, even as a player at 49, the sheer joy of playing. Young kids should try multiple sports and should play them as long as the can.

Kara Lang, who later went on to play for Canada's national team, played for her province in both soccer and basketball when I first coached her in 1999-2000 as head coach of the Ontario provincial team. We worked with her basketball commitments so she could continue to do both. She was not placed in a difficult situation or forced to make a difficult choice between one sport and another. As a result she was a happier young athlete who was left to get on with what was most important, enjoying herself in both her sporting passions.

Challenge yourself as a coach. Make your program a choice. Give players and their families the freedom to enjoy vacations and other important events together. Sign a few more extra players so you have a larger roster to accommodate this for everyone. It should not matter if your star centre forward is away for a game. After all, your role is to develop players, not to win games or trophies. Besides if all players are played in different positions then you will not have one star centre forward but several talented young players capable of playing that position! (See page 106 for more benefits of developing multi-positional players.)

When other training or camp opportunities come up advise players to go and take advantage of these if you feel that it would improve them. And if an opportunity comes along of your players to move on to play at a higher level, encourage them, help them and give yourself a pat on the back. You have helped another young player along the path to be better. You have done your job with this young player and then you can go looking for the next ones to propel forward.

Development versus Winning: The battle for the soul of North American Youth Soccer

North America will always struggle to develop world class players as long as playing competitive games continues to take priority over training. For all the strides that we have made in North America with the implementation of several elite-standards-based leagues (with a focus on development) youth soccer remains insanely competitive. As Diane Scavuzzo, editor of *SoccerNation News*, outlined in a recent article, "the infighting in the high fashion world and even the movie industry pale in comparison to that in youth soccer."

We witness examples of this every week. Our academy trains young players in Burlington, Ontario on Monday, Tuesday and Thursday evenings and we constantly face the challenge of competitive teams invading our training area. Our training ends at 7 pm but by 6 pm we typically have competitive team coaches and officials striding across our training area pleading the usual refrain, "But we have a game!"

I usually give the standard response that we are training our young players and will be of the field promptly at 6:55 pm as per our permit.

This seems to always result in the usual protest again: "But we have a game." The next comment usually goes along the same lines also. "Who are you guys? An academy? Do you have a permit? "When I take time out from coaching our players to assure them that yes, we are an academy and that yes, we have actually been professional enough in our approach to secure a field permit, the negotiations begin. At that point I get an insight into how important the game is to these club officials, how important the points are for the league table and how important it is for their players to warm up properly. They then start surveying our training area to point out which areas they would like use to complete their warm-up. There is no thought given to the young players, as young as five, who are currently on the field. And there is no appreciation for the families of these players who prefer to have their children participate in a non-competitive environment based on long-term development versus the next quick fix of winning a game.

When I point out that there is a whole field vacant about 400 metres away, or a grass area on the far side of the field, just outside the gate, we usually get a frustrated sigh and a comment or two about the unfairness of it all. The most humorous response by one coach was that his players would not be "used to" the other field. We're still not sure how he or his players handle the uncertainly of playing away from home or even changing sides at half time! As the summer has progressed the battle lines have been drawn, the exchanges have become more and more hostile and to be honest it makes me worry about the future of the sport in this continent.

In a world where we can click on a button and see the latest training sessions from top professional club academies in Europe, scan 150 page documenting the best practice development models of Europe's best academies (the "Report on Youth Academies in Europe" from the European Club Association) we can no longer argue ignorance. We know that Bayern Munich (the current Champions League holders) play 7v7 at their 7 to 10 ages levels. We know that the majority of youth academies in Europe have U12 players playing 22-26 games per year (50-60 minutes length), with a training ratio of 3 sessions week/game. The information is at our fingertips, and it can only be that we as a continent — for whatever reason — have so far decided not to follow a youth development model which stresses ensuring that all the young players we interact with become better players and better young people also.

Until quality training sessions are recognized as the best method to develop young players (over games) we will continue to struggle. We're very good at having the best uniforms, wearing bright 300-dollar soccer shoes, having last names on the back of the player shirts like the English Premiership players and packing over-stressed coaches, managers and parents along the sidelines. But we are much less successful at developing talented young players who can go to play at the highest standards of the game.

Attend one of our training sessions at the start and you will see young players with a ball at their feet learning new skills in a positive learning environment. If you stay around until the competitive teams turn up then you will witness a herd of players, coaches and parents stressed beyond belief and striving relentlessly towards the Holy Grail — the next 3 points. Where it takes these players I'm not really sure but what I do know is that the atmosphere that I witness at the end of our training sessions when competitive teams arrive cannot encourage player development. We have now taken the approach to close the gate and protect our young players and families from this environment. The message from us is simple now — respect our training area and we will be off the field promptly at 6:55pm.

The top players in the world play without fear. Messi, Ronaldo, Xavi, Inesta and Ozil could as easily be playing with their mates on the streets around their house when you watch them play. Yes, they are professionals and are paid to help their teams win games but they don't play like that. They play like they have no cares in the world, and, most importantly, they play like they enjoy it.

When I look into the eyes of many young players today they are frightened to make mistakes. They walk onto the field devoid of emotion and being asked to play for so many other people than themselves — their parents, their coach, their club and their teammates, and maybe even that scout in the stands. If we as coaches and parents can remove that pressure and our competitive systems can reduce the impact of games by not posting results or standings up until at least U14 then maybe we can give the young players back their love of the game. Competitive sports in North America have taken a wrong turn towards placing enormous pressure on the shoulders of our young players.

It's time for us to remove that. Let's start by respecting and celebrating when young players are on a field with a ball at their feet, learning new skills. They should not have to play second fiddle to anyone!

Make training fun
and player-centric
to develop
creative players

Summer, 2013: I have just returned from coaching at the Wolves FC North American camp in Rome, Georgia. At the four-day residential camp I had the pleasure of working alongside Gareth Prosser, the Wolves FC academy director from the UK, and his excellent staff. When I returned home one of the first emails I received was from Steve Bottjer at Red Nation Online (*www.rednationonline.ca*) asking me what my thoughts were on the recent performance of the Canadian national men's team at the 2013 Gold Cup. I had to be honest with Steve and say that I had missed the games as I was coaching. But after listening to Steve's re-cap of our team's performance in the tournament, in which our men lost to Martinique and Mexico and drew with Panama, and failed to score a goal the entire tournament, I could only conclude that the common themes are once again at the forefront of our national men's team program: We cannot retain possession very well and have insufficient players at that level who excel technically and can offer creative solutions on the field.

The question made me reflect upon the last few weeks. During that time 1v1 have hosted a Wolves FC player ID camp in Burlington, Ontario for 70 players. From this, 15 players were invited to the national camp. The Wolves staff have commented upon the good technical skills by displayed by North American players but also on the challenges they face when under pressure from opponents or when they have to solve problems for themselves and find creative solutions. What struck me most about watching the Wolves coaching staff in action was how many times they openly discussed adding an element of fun and enjoyment to the sessions. A key consideration in the lesson planning was: "Will he players be engaged and enjoy the session?"

That may seem like an obvious goal when coaches plan training sessions but on many occasions that is not the case. On many occasions training becomes "coach-centric" instead of "player-centric" and sessions are designed because they are "coach favorites" or are easier for the coaching staff to manage, rather than being effective for the players being taught.

The Wolves coaches believe strongly that to learn effectively, young players must be enjoying what they are doing. (Somehow, just writing that sentence, it seems like an obvious point!) The coaches from the UK also believe that young players must enjoy variety in their training and need to be challenged to solve different scenarios on the field. In small-sided games they changed the rules every 4 to 5 minutes (for example, moving from one-touch to two-touches to unlimited touches on the ball) to challenge the players to think for themselves on the field to achieve positive outcomes. On the last day a chipping contest was added as part of the warm up. It was very challenging technically but when players were divided into teams and it

was made into a competition, the players' enjoyment level —
and the resulting tempo of play — immediately went up. The
youngsters were engaged and loved every minute of it. The
coaches reviewed the key points with the players after every
round of competition and the least successful team was required
to sing a song to the other groups… which only added a fun
element to the activity. (I do have to add a note of caution here
— coaches should always ensure that these things remain light-
hearted and are never humiliating.)

When I look at a lot of young North American players
in action, to be honest, they look frightened. Frightened to
make mistakes, even frightened to stand out and be the most
dominant player on the field. This mode of "playing scared"
simply cannot be right. The pressure and the need for results
smother our best young plays and they are frightened to fail.
Our young players play too many competitive games and
have to deal with the expectation levels placed upon them by
coaches and their families.

If we want to see creative and skillful players develop in
North America we have to change our mentality. Coaches and
parents have to ensure that first and foremost the players are
having fun and enjoying themselves. We can't be "on" them
at every practice session and game to perform, and we have to
get away from the win-at-all-costs mentality. It takes away the
opportunity to try things, experiment and play. Let's encourage
them to do their tricks and laugh with friends. Let them come
up with creative solutions rather than rehearse predictable
movements that we think are best for them. Maybe then we
can bring through creative players who think for themselves,
are not frightened to fail and have a passion to play the game
as if they were playing with their friends outside in the park.
After all, one of the best sports quotes I've found comes from
Carin Jennings Gabarra, the 1991 World Champion and 1996

Olympic Gold Medalist with the US women's national soccer team, who said that "a champion is someone who trains when no one is watching."

Another important aspect of having young players try things for themselves and not play in an "over-scripted" way is to consider what might happen when a player gets out of a tightly-controlled environment and is forced to think and play independently — such as when he or she attends a pro trial or a college scouting camp. What will happen when the usual coach, teammates and overall "environment" is suddenly not there?

At our training sessions I have sometimes asked parents not to attend when I feel that they are placing too much expectation or pressure upon the players. If sons or daughters are looking over at their parents for direction or an element of approval then I make the call to give the players some "space" to learn and develop away from prying eyes. It has worked well for our players and the parents themselves have now gotten into a routine where the majority now drop their children of and go grab a coffee and enjoy some downtime themselves. (Talk about a win-win situation!) Our players now are there for themselves. They have taken on greater responsibility for their own development and are progressing at their own pace, rather than the pace at which someone else has decided for them. And as I've mentioned before, if a parent can drop his or her child off at any program, and can leave them there with confidence, they've chosen the right program.

It's important to realize that in training, doing the same actions over and over again simply produces the same results. We, as coaches and parents, can help break the cycle. Make training fun and enjoyable, and facilitate a development environment in which players learn from trying things and making mistakes. Let's be honest: How many times have we, even as adults, learned to do something correctly on our first try? Are we perfect and operating at 100 percent every day at our jobs? I can only speak for myself and say that I have most success when I jump in and try things, make lots of mistakes, and eventually figure things out. I don't think I should be placed in charge of nuclear reactors anytime soon with this method of learning, but it does work when you're working alongside young players who at looking to learn to improve their soccer skills.

The bottom line is this: As coaches and parents, always remember to ask the question " will be players be engaged, and will they enjoy an activity?"

If the answer is "yes", everything else should fall into line after that.

Success through
play-based learning

There are several reasons often given to explain the lack of North American players at the highest levels of the game. One of the main ones is that the fragmented professional levels of the game in Canada and the US, which leads to a lack of professional playing opportunities. If a young child is good at basketball, football or baseball, the argument goes, they have traditional and progressive pathways to higher levels of play and so are much more motivated to excel. However, I think our level of coaching and the type of work we do at the younger levels has an equally serious impact the abilities of players we are producing.

Most coaching drills that I have seen in North American soccer are, in my opinion, designed to achieve repetition and prompt a standard action from players. However the flaw in this method of coaching is that the game is not "standard" — it is in fact entirely random! To play at the highest levels young players must be able to react successfully to chaotic events thrown at them on a field of play. Therefore they should train to cope with random events that are game-specific. This can be achieved by teaching players in small-sided games or putting them in activities that are more game-realistic.

For example, to teach fast transition from attack to defense a coach can have the team that just scored a goal turn around immediately and attack the opposite goal. That way the game has totally changed. Players in advanced attacking positions will immediately be in defensive positions and players previously defending will now be attacking. If we can increasingly place our young players in these types of "chaos" scenarios on the field then they will have had more opportunities to experience the changing nature of games and the randomness of the patterns of play. Unlike basketball, football or baseball, set plays make up such a low percentage of overall play in soccer that we must develop young players capable of thinking for themselves and successfully solving situations on the field of play.

After returning from a recent Wolves FC national camp in Georgia (Summer, 2013) where Wolves FC academy coaches introduced several different conditions to players within small sided games, I tried the same with several 1v1 Soccer academy groups. The players responded very well. The tempo of play went up and they excelled in an ever-changing, fast-paced environment. I kept introducing new conditions every 3 or 4 minutes to keep the players thinking all the time how best to succeed within the current match conditions. For example, a game started with restrictions on how advanced players had to be to score a goal, so I placed a 10 yard "scoring zone line" across the field in front of both goals. Then I introduced a condition that if a team scored, they immediately attacked the opposite goal. To add a fun element to the play I introduced kick-ins (as opposed to throw-ins) with the rule that you had to keep your right hand on the ball when you kicked it in. I knew that players would inevitably forget this and it became a source of amusement every time someone forgot this and conceded the kick in to the opposite team. Obviously, learning to kick a ball with your hand on it is a skill with very limited application in "real" soccer — but the mental discipline of learning to adapt to a new condition is a huge part of developing in the game.

When the pattern of play became too direct and central I then introduced a new condition that goals must be scored from wide positions. The attacking team had to play a pass wide and outside the regular lines of play for an overlapping player to deliver a cross. Once the players adapted and began to enjoy success playing with this condition I then introduced the condition that a goal must be scored on one touch from the delivered cross. By the time the game ended the players were managing 5 or 6 different conditions, each layered on top on one another. The play was fast-paced, dynamic, competitive and it was clear that the players were enjoying it — and to any outside observer, it was fantastic to watch!

As a player or coach you always know when a session has gone really well. Time flies by quickly. No sooner have you tied your boots up than you are taking them off again. Introducing different conditions to small-sided games in quick succession will stimulate the minds of your young players and foster creative play. Give some thought to a series of conditions that best matches the age and skill level of your players and try this at your next session.

Your players will enjoy it, your parents won't complain that "the coach just runs the same drills over and over"... and most importantly, you will provide your young players with greater experience at thinking quickly for themselves during random play.

The importance of self -motivation in becoming a top player

A recent interview with Arsène Wenger, manager of the top-flight English club Arsenal, outlined the importance of young players learning to be "consistently motivated" in order to play at the highest levels of the game.

In his typically thoughtful style, Wenger defined a motivated person as "someone who has the capacity to recruit the resources to complete a goal." He then gave an example of how he got lost jogging in Japan. He explained how he was motivated to come back to the hotel but could not find his way back. He could have hailed a taxi but as a sportsman he was determined to find a solution himself and find his own way back. In summary, Wenger believes that when you look at people who are successful they are the ones who are consistently motivated and always willing to made sacrifices to achieve their goals.

This mirrors what I see at our academy at 1v1 Soccer. We have had players join our program at various ages and abilities. The ones I focus I most on and believe will go on to play at higher levels are the ones who are determined to truly make themselves players. During training, they simply get on with it. They train like it will be their last session and are constantly on the edge during our technical warm-ups, trying new things and not being content with their current level of skill.

When we play small-sided games and constantly change conditions, they are the players quickly working out how to succeed within the changing environment. They are the players who are capable of playing at a high level themselves but also inspiring and helping other players around them. In football (soccer) your teammates are the best judge of your performance. Despite what parents and even coaches see on the sidelines, teammates are the ones who truly know if you're making yourself available for passes, making runs off the ball into open space, changing the point of attack based on what the opposition is doing, making tracking runs back to assist the defence and able to produce something a little different when the pressure is on.

Players and their parents do not often realize how much coaches learn about players when you observe them off the field. Are they mixing well socially, do they carry their own boots and training bag, do they tie their own laces? These behaviors can all be indicators of how self-motivated players are and can give a very good idea of whether or not take responsibility for preparation themselves. Do players ask questions during training to the coaching staff as they try to understand instructions? Can they work things out for themselves, solve problems, and are they determined to overcome obstacles?

Think of the last time you truly had to work out something by yourself. Maybe you had a flat tire, your lawnmower was not working or you just could not get in touch with your boss to make an important decision. We've likely all been in those situations where we have had to work things out for ourselves and have had no other options. Chances are you probably exceeded your own expectations of yourself and successfully resolved the issue. You probably also felt a surge of pride and confidence in accomplishing that.

That is exactly the type of feeling that we should be trying to instill in our young players. Parents and coaches can both contribute to this. Parents can give young players the responsibility of checking on their training times and game schedules, emailing the coach if they cannot make a practice or game. The players can be responsible for packing their own equipment and water, carrying their own training bag and tying their own laces. Coaches can help by giving players the responsibility for warm-up, taking care of equipment and even providing them the responsibility to think up and organize the small-sided game at the end of practice.

As a player gets older, this approach becomes more and more important. One of our 1v1 players recently attended a camp at a US university, where she learned from the coaching staff that if a parent sends an email to a coach inquiring about the team's program and showing interest in their daughter being recruited, that player's name goes to the "bottom of the list" — since those coaches are only interested in dealing with players who take the initiative on their own, and not with potentially intrusive parents.

We have many good technical young players in North America. If they can marry good technique with consistent motivation as outlined by Wenger then we can expect great things from our young players. If we shelter them from decision-making and responsibility on and off the field, my fear is that we will develop skillful young players who will struggle later on with the skill-sets they will need to overcome the inevitable set-backs that elite sport will throw their way.

Let's teach young players to be determined, demanding of themselves to improve and to be consistent with it. If young players can do that, they might just be having a chat with Mr. Wenger one day.

My starting 11 —
All-time and current

Like any young lad growing up in Northern Ireland in the 1970s a significant amount of my time was spent picking "starting 11s" — that is, imaginary "dream team" lineups — in my head. I would pick starting 11s for my favourite teams Linfield, Arsenal and Rangers and even through their managers at the time never did give me a call prior to the matches on Saturdays to seek advice, I was always fully prepared to take the call and provide my thoughts.

When I had finished those line-ups I then moved on to the really interesting ones such as the Northern Ireland national teams, and the all-time lineups for Linfield, Rangers and Arsenal. Just as a side note, this is a universal pastime among soccer fans the world over, and the excellent English magazine FourFourTwo has a regular back-page feature in which a famous manager or player is asked to pick their dream team, sometimes with conditions attached. (For example, an Arsenal legend of yore was recently asked to pick his dream team but could not include any Arsenal players.) In truth, nothing much has changed today, except my wife gets to make fun of me and remind me that this type of behaviour was never outlined in our marriage contract. (I still maintain that all this was clearly outlined in the fine print.)

I must admit that it was much easier to pick all-time starting 11s when I was 11, versus nearing my 50th birthday. There are many more players eligible. But with that in mind, here goes my favourite all-time starting 11. I've included explanations as, of course, I'm overlooking many great players.

Goalkeeper: Pat Jennings (Northern Ireland)

Maybe a surprise and I can be accused of being biased towards a fellow countryman but I remember standing on the spying kop at Windsor Park during Northern Ireland games and thinking that he would never be beaten. Inevitably he was, as we were not a very good team back then, but I can't remember one mistake that he made as a goalkeeper. He was calm, controlled his box, good with his feet and would radiate confidence when he caught the ball with one hand. He also was one of the first goalkeepers to use his legs and feet and stop shots in an unconventional way. Voted Player of the Year in 1973 by the Football Writers Association for the old First Division in England, and went on to play a long and distinguished career for Spurs, Arsenal and Northern Ireland.

Right Full-Back: Carlos Alberto (Brazil)

The captain and right full back for the great Brazilian team of the 1970 World Cup. (Yes, there was a dream team prior to Barcelona!) Was one on the first attacking full-backs to get up and down the wing and arrive late in the opposition's box to score goals or create opportunities for others. A wonderful athlete with good technical skills. Who can forget his marvelous final goal in the 1970 World Cup Final!

Left Full-Back: Paolo Maldini (Italy)

It is difficult not to select any Italian defenders. They have had many great players along the back line down the years and I've selected one of the best in Maldini. Completely two-footed, he could play either left full-back or as a central defender. He was a great servant to AC Milan and played 25 seasons in one of the world's top leagues — Serie A. He was such a great competitor and as I mentioned he had the mindset of all the great Italian defenders. He was also comfortable going forward but is in my side here for his consistency at the highest level for so many years and his great defensive qualities. It is also worth noting that his dad, Cesare, was an outstanding coach and player.

Central Defender: Franz Beckenbauer (Germany)

Beckenbauer defined the role of "sweeper" during the 1970's and was confident on the ball to carry it into midfield and launch attacks. Earlier in his career he had played in central midfield and this experience benefited him as he redefined the central defender role to the position we know today as sweeper. He was a great organizer on the field, as witnessed by his nickname, The Kaiser, and had great vision. I often recount the story (which I read in an interview) to our young players of his ability to close his eyes and know exactly where every one of his teammates was at any one time. What a tremendous attribute for young players to aspire to.

Central Defender: Vincent Kompany (Belgium)

Kompany is such an imposing figure as a centre back and like all the players in this side, a great competitor. One of the few on my list who is a currently active player, he was captain of a Man City side that clawed back a large points lead from Manchester United to win the 2011/2012 English premiership title. Big players deliver on big occasions and his winning goal at the Etihad Stadium against United in what was his club's biggest game in 40 years said much for his character. A decisive header in a crowded area demonstrated his bravery and will to win, two important qualities as a central defender. Kompany's physical presence together with Beckenbauer's reading of the game would be difficult to get past.

Central Midfield: Patrick Vieira (France)

Maybe a surprise choice but every great team needs a balance of personalities and attributes. Playing Vieira in central midfield would provide protection to the back four defensively. He was a key player in Arsenal's Invincibles team that went the whole season in the English Premier League unbeaten in 2003-2004, which is an astonishing record. Vieira had both defensive and attacking qualities and was more than capable of providing protection to his more skilled colleagues should the opposition wish for a battle. The type of midfield player every great team needs, mobile, rarely lost possession and a fierce competitor who realized the challenge of taking full control of the important midfield area.

Central Midfield: Zinedine Zidane (France)

It came down to a difficult choice between Zidane and his countryman Michel Platini to be the creative force in my all-France central midfield. Both were the best players in Europe of their generation. Both could control the tempo of play during a game but Zidane for me was slightly better and more disciplined as a team player. He rarely lost the ball and his tight control got him out of many tight situations. Could set up others and score himself and his range and vision of passing would be a great asset to this team.

Right-Wing: George Best (Northern Ireland)

I had the pleasure of watching Best live during the early 1970s when he was at his prime and carrying the entire Manchester United team on his back. I blame this excess of responsibility for his early retirement at the highest levels. Wonderfully gifted with both feet, an athlete, a fierce competitor and had the imagination to do things with the ball no one had even thought of yet. He also played in an era where defenders had full licence to kick lumps out of opponents. Best was the best player in Europe if not the world by age 21. Not bad for someone who was told that he was too small as a youngster. He did not have the advantage of playing in World Cup finals with Northern Ireland (they didn't qualify during his era) but in my opinion he was simply the best ever. In my dream scenario, he may start on the right wing but I wouldn't restrict him to that position. The team would respond to his movement and provide the proper cover if the team lost the ball and he was out of position. Best would also move inside to combine with central midfielders and forwards to create space for Carlos Alberto's over-lapping runs on the right wing.

Left-Wing: Cristiano Ronaldo (Portugal)

Cristiano Ronaldo does not always receive the credit that his play deserves due to his brash personality but he would be in the team on merit. He arrived at Manchester United behind players such as Wayne Rooney but through his strong dedication to improve he has made himself the current best player in the world. Great feet and pace are big strengths as is ability to score with his head. Despite his sometimes flashy approach, Ronaldo is also considered one of the hardest-working players in training on his Real Madrid team. With Best on the right wing and Ronaldo on the left we would get the ball to these two at every opportunity. Both players would be capable of beating defenders in 1v1s and getting in behind defenses to deliver crosses or cutting inside for shooting opportunities. Both would be a real handful for the opposition. I did think about playing Dutch legend Johan Cruyff in this position but I like my wide players to have real pace... so Ronaldo gets the nod.

Forward: Diego Maradonna (Argentina)

Maradonna or Messi? You really can't go wrong with either Argentinian for the number 10 role but I've selected Maradonna. He led an average national team to the World Cup in 1986 and inspired an even weaker Argentinian side to the World Cup Final in 1990. On top of that he led Napoli to back-to-back league titles in Italy 1986/87 and 1989/90. He also played in an era where defenders could tackle much more aggressively and when forwards did not enjoy the advantages they do today with offside decisions. Could Barcelona win league titles without Messi? Possibly. Could Napoli or Argentinia have achieved their success without Maradonna? I don't think so! A wonderful talent, he had close control, pace, balance, a good football brain and like all players in this team a tremendous will to win. The 2nd goal he scored against England in the quarter final of the 1986 World Cup — not the hand-of-God goal; the other one where he dribbled past the entire England side — was the best goal I've seen .

Forward : Ronaldo Luis Nazario de Lima (Brazil)

Difficult choices again but as a manager you have to make these types of decisions for the benefit of the team. Do you pick the Brazilian Pele, Cruyff or Van Basten of the Netherlands (amongst others) as the number 9? I've decided on Ronaldo (the Brazilian one). In his prime, he was unplayable with his pace and direct play right to goal. Would thrive on the supply

from Zidane and Maradonna centrally and the crosses from
Best and the other Ronaldo out wide. His record for most goals
scored at World Cup finals (15) confirms his finishing ability
and playing in this team he would have many opportunities.
Like all the best number 9s also capable of creating and
finishing his own chances.

In summary, I had a great time thinking about and picking
this team. My mother asked who would manage the team and
I replied in a flash — me! There is no way that I would pass
on the wonderful opportunity to manage this team. Truth is I
would only have to throw the ball out onto the field and tell
them to get on with it!

So you want to be a coach: How to develop your own coaching philosophy

I'm not sure how many coaches sit down, reflect on their own coaching philosophy, and then put their thoughts down in writing. This was something that I did as part of my early coaching education. Back then, you were required to take courses (in the NCCP, or National Coaching Certification Program) that were based upon the theory of coaching in all sports, together with your own sport's specific courses. I thought that this was a tremendous introduction for new coaches, as you had the opportunity to study alongside coaches from many different sports and learn new ideas, that you could use to solve similar issues within your own sport.

It was a great advantage for me to draft my own coaching philosophy before I started because it gave me a set of values, beliefs and principles that I could consistently apply to the various situations I've faced over the years. I have used my coaching philosophy to arrive at decisions on how to deal with players, parents, colleagues and organizations I've worked for or alongside. Central to any coaching philosophy should be the values and behaviours you wish to impart upon your players . They are, after all, a reflection of your work, and I always get satisfaction in hearing that "he or she is a true 1v1 player," even when it involves them overrunning the ball and losing it trying to be creative on the field. Not everyone appreciates this trait but it is central to our coaching philosophy at 1v1: challenge yourself and push the boundaries to find out how good you can be.

In an effort to help new coaches develop their own coaching philosophy I want to share a helpful document by Bo Hanson, a 4 time Olympian in rowing from Australia, and a well-known coaching consultant. (http://www.athleteassessments. com/coachphil). Hanson outlines a 5-step process listed below which can help all aspiring coaches, or even experienced coaches develop their own coaching philosophy statement. Here's my summary, with some of my own examples added in:

Step 1: What is most important to you in your coaching role?
These values represent things that are not negotiable for you and should define the main objectives in your coaching. What are you trying to achieve? Hanson has several questionnaires that will help you communicate your values. They may be random thoughts at the moment or values you have used for years but have never sat down and documented. Either way, the questionnaires by Hanson may help. I did not complete these questionnaires when first developing my own coaching philosophy but what was important to me in all my coaching roles was that I was developing players who would be capable of playing the game with skill, creativity, vision and passion. Rather than coach players to win things I was more interested in helping players to develop to play at higher levels of the

game. I have always had strong opinions on how best to achieve this and knew early on that I wanted to have a high level of autonomy in my work so that I could implement my own beliefs with no limits or interference from others.

Step 2: Learn from your own experiences

This is an important step as it lets you reflect upon your own experiences as a player and even as a coach. My own thought is because you continue to learn every day, as a coach and as a person, as you face new experiences, you should be sure to sit down every year and review your coaching philosophy statement to add to or refine it. Over the years I have done this with my own statement. The core values and principles have not changed but my work in putting it into play has changed in order to communicate it better and I have added to it.

Step 3: What is your own coaching style?

Every coach should have a style that reflects their own personality. When I was seeking advice from experienced coaches, prior to becoming a coach, the best advice I received (and I received it on more than one occasion) was to be yourself and don't try to be someone you are not — because your players will quickly see through this.

Hanson believes that is important that coaches understand and be secure with their own coaching style so that we are better positioned to adapt to different situations. As I've mentioned earlier, coaches should be "player-centric" in their approach. He identifies 4 distinct coaching styles (Conscientious/Dominance/Steady/Influence) which should all be demonstrated for the most effective coaching — depending upon the situation you face.

Most coaches have no problem demonstrating the "dominance" traits which are results- and authority-based but you will face situations with players that will require "steady" attributes that involve being relaxed and a good listener. The "art" of coaching is to know when to use which approach, given the situation you place.

For more information on the four distinct levels of coaching see   *www.athleteassessments.com/articles/understanding_four_coaching_styles_sport.html*

Step 4: Discover your coaching philosophy

This step is when you review the information from the previous steps and document the behaviour you wish to exhibit consistently, how you wish to conduct yourself and how this behavior impacts on your athletes. This is a good opportunity to document how you wish to measure success in your coaching endeavours.

Again, Hanson provides many questionnaire templates that can be used to help document this.

Step 5: Keep it visible and alive

This is the final step in the process where you are encouraged to complete your coaching philosophy statement, keep it visible to both you and your players, and incorporate your findings into your everyday coaching life.

I would recommend that all coaches download the assessment guide free at www.athleteassessments.com and take a moment to complete the exercises to either develop your first coaching philosophy statement or refine your existing one.

I have enclosed mine below as a sample to help with the exercise.

My Coaching Philosophy — Ian McClurg

Success for me as a coach is to develop young players who can play the game with skill, creativity, vision and passion and help them to transition to higher levels of play. It is also important that the players that I work with develop good life skills and become good people who are humble, take responsibility for themselves and demonstrate respect for themselves, their colleagues and their family.

My coaching philosophy towards development is based in inspiring young players to be the best that they can be. This can best be achieved when we remember that football (soccer) is a game. It is not about wins and losses. It is about teaching young players to be open to learning, having the courage to try new things and challenging themselves to becoming better and to find new solutions.

I accomplish this by maximizing contact on the ball and teaching the players how to make their own decisions through small-sided games.

I have strong beliefs on the type of training and the environment required to accomplish these goals. It is important for me to have autonomy over the type of coaching work I do and to continually challenge myself to improve both as a coach and person in the work that I do.

Tips for pre-game, half-time and post-game team talks for youth players

Before the game, at half-time and after the game youth coaches have key opportunities to provide feedback to their group in terms of game performance. During these occasions, I like to keep things as simple as possible for young players. I will have the players arrive and report to me one hour before the game so their preparation is relaxed and they are not rushing. It gives the group a chance to meet up, have a chat with their friends and start to prepare for the game. We try to follow the same routine for the warm-up and have one of the players lead the players through this. This helps transition the group from chatting with their friends to starting to prepare their bodies to play.

Pre-game team talks should be brief and delivered at the appropriate time. For me, the best time to deliver the team-talk is about 30 minutes prior to the game for younger players (under age 12) and around 40 minutes prior to kick-off for the older players. The players will have already worked through a series of physical (light jogging and dynamic stretching exercises) plus some technique work (1 ball per player or in small groups)

My team talks consist of using discs on the ground so that the players can all see the team shape we are trying to achieve when in possession of the ball and when we are not in possession of the ball. I then announce the starting line-up. If there are any major changes to this from previous games or I feel that a certain player will get down or disappointed by not starting then I will have already pulled them aside, explained the decision and put a positive spin on things. All players in our academy squads play a minimum of 50 percent of game time, so I make sure they understand that they will get playing time and a chance to play. If they are not starting due to a lack of commitment in training recently, then I might issue them a little challenge like, "Show us what you are all about today. Be the best player on the field today."

The instructions to the team are kept simple as our philosophy is to have a good week of training prior to the game where we will have communicated how we wish to play. Generally speaking I give the team three objectives for attacking and then three objectives when we are defending. For older teams I will also touch upon our goals during transition from attack to defence and vice versa. For attacking objectives these can be as simple as playing at a higher tempo than our opponents and keeping the ball moving or playing down the wings and to get 5 quality crosses into their box within the first 10 attempts. Defensively, we could work on winning the ball back within 6 seconds of losing it.

These instructions give the players focus as a group, and the more measurable our aims, the better. The instructions are always positive and focused on our own performance levels, not on what the other team might be intending to do. Our objective as an academy team is to develop players, not win games, so we focus on the level of performance of the group. I will end the team talk with statements like "this is how we will have success playing today" and even deliver a catch-phrase that best captures our objectives that day.

As a coach, you also have to judge the mood of the group at that moment. If they are anxious or nervous then you can use humour to lighten things up and relax the players. If they are overly confident or not focused sometimes to will have to deliver your message and communicate in a more business-like fashion where they will all understand the need to sharpen their focus. In situations like this, a coach`s body language and non-verbal cues are sometimes as important as the words he or she uses. Something as simple as extra hand gestures to emphasize the importance of a point, or pointing a finger a player to stress the key role he or she will play can go a long way.

When I coached the Ontario provincial team all our players taped a certain saying or set of instructions to their wrist to provide focus on what the team objective was that day. This kind of thing develops camaraderie amongst the group and is a very powerful technique to use for high-performance teams.

After the team talk our players will engage in a series of small-sided games designed to sharpen their touch and decision-making. It is during this period that I may pull certain players aside for individual instructions. If a player has been suffering a lapse in confidence, does not seem as positive and up for the game or is nervous then I will chat with them in an effort to get them into a more positive state of mind.

During our academy games we may have one half-time or two breaks in play to communicate with the group. The pre-game instructions that I delivered before the game provide the framework for evaluation during the game. I will make notes alongside the three attacking and three defensive objectives we set and also some general comments that may be relevant outside these objectives. The half-time team talk is again brief and to the point. I let the players settle, take drinks on board and relax first. Then I will touch upon three things (attacking or defensively) that we have done very well. After that I will touch upon three things that we can improve upon. I try to give as specific examples as possible and may use the discs on the ground again to communicate how our team shape should be. I will ask the group as a whole or even individuals specifically what they are seeing during the game so that the players are encouraged to think about the game and be part of providing solutions.

I will leave them with one general theme before they go back on the field again. If things have gone well, I ask if we can we push on and move to a higher level. Or if we have struggled we will dismiss the previous period of play and start again with the score at 0-0 in our minds for the next period with the objective of improving our performance levels.

Again, it is important to judge the overall mood of the group. As I have mentioned I don't like our players to get too carried away emotionally either way in the middle of a game, so if they are overly-confident I will be a little more critical on details and challenge them to improve further and if they are lacking confidence this is then an opportunity to build confidence. One of the most effective methods to achieve this is to go around the players individually and tell the entire group what attributes that player will be demonstrating in the next period of play. For example, I might say "John is great at getting forward from his right back position and will be getting down the wing during the next period to deliver lots of dangerous crosses. "

This achieves two things: It raises the confidence of the individual player by highlighting a strength in front of his or her peers and for the group, it paints a positive image in their heads of how the team can be successful when they go back on the field. It is a very powerful technique that I picked up watching Crewe Alexandra academy coaches in the UK speaking to players. As a team there is nothing more inspiring than having all of your players run onto the field confident and looking forward to playing.

After the game, the players will shake hands with the opposition and officials and begin their cool-down. It is a chance for them to wind down from the rigors of a game and relax and at the same time start the recovery process for their bodies. We then meet as a group to summarize briefly the performance. Again, this should be positive and should focus on the accomplishments by the group during the game.

Sometimes I will ask the group how they think they did with respect to our game objectives so that they have a chance to put their thoughts across. It is important to verify that you as a coach are in touch with the group on how they are feeling and this also engages the players in thinking how they played and taking on ownership for the performance.

If we have really struggled with something during the game then I will point out that we have much work to do in that area but that we will work through it in training and that I'm confident that through hard-work and perseverance we can improve. If we have experienced a bad result and I feel that the players may be overly criticized on the way home by parents or siblings then I like to spend extra time pointing out the positives, downplaying the actual result. For example, I may say "yes, it took us longer to get going today but we tied the last period and proved we can compete at this level. Now, we have to show consistency. Don't get too down regarding the result, think about what you did well today and don't let anyone take away from you what you have done well today. We will work out the rest in training".

At a National Soccer Coaches Association of America convention I once listened to Steve Highway, Liverpool's Academy director at the time, speak about the most damage (in his words) that was done to young players within the first 45 minutes after a game when parents or others (besides the coaching staff) had an opportunity to counter the instructions or feedback that had been given to young players. As a result, Liverpool academy had kept their young players together as a group and in the change-room for 45 minutes after the game, for a chance to de-brief players with the right kind of information. I have always remembered this statement and to be honest I do fear the contradictory instructions that our young players do receive away from the training field. It is important that parents support their children and provide an ear to listen to or even put their arm around their shoulder when things are not going so well. This is much more helpful than providing contradictory advice to that delivered by coaches and only succeeds in confusing players and making them less confident in their actions.

Keep your team-talks brief, to the point and inspire your young players to aspire to be better. Be in tune with the overall mood of the group so you can tailor your message and tone accordingly. Be positive with at least 90 percent of your comments and provide solutions on how to improve performance when you are being critical. Don't underestimate the power of speaking to players individually when giving instructions or galvanizing the group (with an objective or even a saying) that makes them feel part of a very powerful group.

As a coach, you will find your own best pre-game, half-time and post-game rituals that are that the most effective for your own players. I hope in some way sharing my own practices can act as at least a guide in this area.

Learning through watching games on television

Young players in North America have the disadvantage of not being able to watch as many professional games in person as their counterparts in Europe. There are only 18 MLS teams spread amongst a population of over 340 million people while in England a population of just over 60 million supports 92 professional teams and several other semi-professional leagues, which play a good standard.

At 1v1, we encourage all our young players to go to as many live games as possible. From our base in southwestern Ontario, the closest professional team is Toronto FC, about 45 minutes away. Luckily, with the advent of TV coverage and the Internet, young players can watch an enormous amount of soccer from overseas, and we encourage our young players to watch as many games on the television as possible.

So what should young players look for when they watch games on television or the internet? What do they look for to increase their game understanding? I have included a list of questions below that can be used by young players and even parents and coaches when watching games. (I was told a long time ago during one of my coaching courses that I would never be able to enjoy a game again as an impartial spectator but would be looking for different things during a game with the new knowledge I had gained. I have to say it is true. You may find the same once you start to analyze the game at a different level.)

Here's a quick breakdown:

Overall Team Analysis

- Team formation i.e. 4-4-2, 4-3-3, 4-2-3-1 etc., and does it change during the game?
- Does the team look to control possession or look to play on the counter-attack?
- Who are the main players standing out when the team is attacking and when defending?

Attacking Patterns when in possession

- Does the team try to play direct to goal with few passes in their build-up play, often hitting balls through the air like Stoke City of the English Premiership for the last few years, or do they move the ball around mostly on the ground, with many passes to create attacking opportunities like Arsenal for example?
- Does the team play at a high tempo like English teams or play at a slower pace like Spanish and Italian sides?
- Does the team try to play down the wings like Sevilla FC in Spain or through the middle like their counterparts Valencia ?
- How many and which players are involved in attacking build-ups?
- Who is the main player that the team plays through in midfield?

- Who is the main player that they look to play in for goal scoring opportunities?
- Do they play passes into space or directly into players?
- How good are the players technically — dribbling, 1v1's, crossing, passing, shooting, first touch control?
- Which players combine frequently? For example when you watch Barcelona Inestia, Xavi and Messi combine many times during attacking play.

Defending Strategy

- Is the defending line deep and close to their own goal or is the defending line high up the field and close to the half-way line? A high line condenses play for the opposition because of the possibility of attackers going offside, but makes team vulnerable to passes over the top and quick players making runs in behind.
- Is the team man-making or using zonal marking? Many teams are now using zonal marking, where defenders mark space, rather than players, versus man-marking at corners for example which has been a new trend in the game during the last few years
- Do all players close space and get involved in defending or just certain players?
- Does the team press the other team by aggressively trying to win the ball back by overloading the team in possession in certain areas of the field?

Change in possession

- How fast does the team transition from attack to defence?
- How fast does the team transition from defence to attack?

- Do they players work as a cohesive unit or does the team look disjointed?
- Does the team attack quickly after regaining possession or do they look to take less risk and maintain possession?
- When losing the ball how quick does the team look to win the ball back and in what areas of the field do they try to do this? For example, during the last few years, Barcelona has looked to win the ball back quickly as high up the field as possible

I hope this summary will provide a general insight into what to look for when watching games on television, the Internet or live. Today, more than ever, an exhaustive set of statistics is available after every game to add to the viewing experience. To check this out you can check out Statszone which is an app that logs and shares statistics from the most popular leagues throughout the world. There are also a lot of good websites that can provide comprehensive analysis of games; one of the best is *www.zonalmarking.net*

As young players build their knowledge of the game this will make them aware of how good players have to be technically to play at the highest levels, and how tactically aware they must be as well. Even watching professional players warm up can be an education for some of our younger players. In the summer of 2013 the top Italian side Roma visited Toronto to play Toronto FC and one of our families commented how impressed they were at how well the Roma players were passing the ball during warm-up, compared to their opponents.

Of course, as a coach I do not want to advocate for a massive amount of screen time for any young person. But as I have explained above, some constructive and thoughtful game watching can pay huge dividends. It is great for young players to aspire to play at the highest levels and to try to emulate skills that they see during professional games. Watching top level matches can also be a great tool for developing greater understanding of what players do when they have the ball and the runs they do and other responsibilities they have off the ball.

Tips for young players attending trials

As players progress in the sport they will face the challenges of attending trials in order to gain selection to play at higher levels. The advice I give to young players in these situations is very simple: Be confident in your own ability and play to your strengths. If you are good at 1v1 situations make sure you look for occasions during games where you can show these skills. Don't let the game pass you by, look to get on the ball and show what you can do.

Young players are understandably nervous during trial situations so it I is important that the people around them, like family and friends, go out of their way to make sure that they are relaxed and not wasting energy leading up to the trial worrying about not making an impression. If young players worry about this, two things generally happen: they become negative in their thinking, and too focused on what might go wrong, versus how they can positively make an impact.

Young players should get lots of rest by going to bed early, even having a nap during the afternoon, if the trial is in the evening. They should hydrate properly and eat the right foods to ensure that they are in peak condition. It is best to keep normal pre-game rituals in place rather than change things. It can also be helpful for young players to watch video (if they have them) of their best performances to build up confidence. Or, if video is not available, then they can replay positive moments during previous games over and over in their minds.

I used to replay great moments that I had watched on television from players I admired in my head. In my mind, I was George Best beating 3 or 4 players on the wing, or in later years Liam Brady spraying passes at will in the Arsenal midfield. I never did reach the heights of these two as players but I managed to trick my mind into believing that I was an athlete of their calibre, to give myself confidence. I tended to play different positions as a young player so if I was playing as a winger then I would replay George Best highlights in my head and if I was playing in central midfield then it was the best plays by Brady or Alan Ball or George Graham that I would play in my head. My grandfather and uncle used to take me to watch Linfield in the Irish league every Saturday, so often I would imagine being Billy Murray, Peter Rafferty or Davie Nixon. I'm not sure if this works for everyone but I often thought of the best moments of these players when playing in trial matches, on the school playground or playing with my mates on the street.

Nowadays young players can watch YouTube videos of all the top players and Messi, Ronaldo, Iniesta, Xavi and other stars have given young players many great examples of how to play the game with skill, creativity, vision and passion. Even watching video highlights on their phone or iPad on the way to the trial can inspire young players and put an extra spring in their step. Some players prefer to play their own music which relaxes them and gives them extra adrenaline depending upon the music. The trick is for all young players to develop their own routines prior to training and games. If they don't know which routines to follow they should think of the best game they played and then try to follow this routine as best they can. Having a routine in place prior to a trial will allow young players to relax as the preparation will be familiar and they will be less inclined to put additional pressure on themselves if they treat it like another practice or game. There are many examples of important cup finals being won by teams who followed their tried and true pre-game preparations rather than change them because the event was more important.

When young players arrive at a trial they should get to the field early to introduce themselves to the coaching staff and offer any assistance with the equipment. They can take the initiative to mix with other players and even set up a game of keep away. Coaches want to see young players be enthusiastic and have a passion for the game. They also want to see young players take initiative both on and off the field. Will they stand around and require direction from the coaching staff or take the initiative themselves to warm up? Young players should understand that they are being evaluated as soon as they set foot out of the car — not just when they are on the field of play.

For example, one of our 1v1 players recently attended a trial with a much older team, and was surprised to discover that while many other players were simply standing around outside the gates to the field — which was occupied by other teams holding their own trials — the coach who would be evaluating her actually expected his players to be warming up on a small patch of grass outside the field so that the minute the field was vacant, his trial could begin.

Trials can be daunting for young players but many make an error in trying to play within themselves to avoid mistakes. There is a fine balance here between not trying to do things you are not capable of, just to try to seem impressive, and playing too safe. Coaches making decisions on players typically choose players who have done something to get noticed rather than rule out players for making mistakes. If players have not taken the initiative to get on the ball and try things it will be hard for them to get identified. Mistakes will inevitably occur but if young players lose the ball in 1 v1 situations then I tell them not to worry about this, simply show the will to win the ball back quickly. If mistakes are made passing, I always recommend to players to keep it simple by making shorter and low risk passes the next few times that they are in possession to regain confidence. If their first touch and timing is not quite as good as usual then find other ways to positively impact the play. Be vocal and encourage teammates, track back to win possession and chase and force mistakes from the opposition to win the ball back for your team.

The skill set and attitude that players have are responsible for gaining them the opportunity to try out. Therefore, they should focus on their strengths as a player. These are the attributes that got them there, so they should play their own game, relax, and more importantly go out to and embrace the challenge and enjoy the occasion. Either way, the experience will make them better players and it is important to remember that there will always more opportunities to show what a good player they are.

The role of formations in youth development

Formation — that is, the way a coach sets up his or her team on the field — can play a positive role in youth development but I do believe that there is too much focus and emphasis placed on this aspect of the game for young people. The focus and emphasis should be on skill development at the younger ages and this work should be completed with players working individually on their skills or in small groups. Teaching an eight year old to play a specific formation, and emphasizing only one position within that set-up, only takes time away from the most important role by a coach at this level — to improve a young players confidence and skill level with a ball.

The great English coach Brian Clough (whose slightly fictionalized life was the subject of the excellent film *The Damned United*) rarely set up his teams with formations. Instead he gave his players specific roles and responsibilities. Clough said that "players lose you games, not tactics. There's so much crap talked about tactics by people who barely know how to win at dominos."

Clough was reflecting on England's exit from the Euro Championship in 2000, but he might have been talking about any youth or professional context. What Clough did make sure about was that he used detail and specific examples for his players to follow. For example, his Nottingham Forest team were told to get the ball on every opportunity to John Robertson on the left wing. When this happened, Martin O'Neill on the opposite wing was asked to be more defensive minded and tuck inside. When Robertson was moving forward on the left wing he essentially became another forward and the Forest formation switched from a 4-4-2 to a 4-3-3. To cite just another example, there is an excellent video on YouTube of Arsenal manager Arsène Wenger, speaking about his formation a few years back. (Unfortunately, for those who don`t speak French it can be a bit hard to understand.) Wenger says that while he was famous for the 4-3-3 set-up at the time, his team very often was actually playing in a 4-1-4-1 formation depending on what was happening on the field. That illustrates part of the reason that I'm a bit skeptical of how much discussion and emphasis is placed on formations in coaching work. In reality the game is random and fluid so it is difficult and in most cases not advised to maintain a rigid formation.

Our youth teams do have a starting formation but we tend more to assign roles and responsibilities rather than placing much emphasis on teaching a rigid structure. For example if our left full back attacks down the flank then we will ask that our right fullback, on the opposite flank, tucks in to provide cover and support to our central defenders so we are able to deal with a quick counter attack. In central midfield one player will be asked to be the link player responsible for receiving the ball from defenders and then combining with the other midfield players and the forwards. The following week that same player or even later during the same game will be given the responsibility to be an advanced midfield player combining more creatively with forwards in more advanced areas of the field.

We believe that assigning players with these types of roles and responsibilities and letting them experience different playing scenarios each week accelerates their understanding of the game. We do not believe in creating specialist players who are only capable of playing one position and repeatedly tell the players that they are not defenders, midfielders or forwards but , simply, "players." Even our young goalkeepers play out on occasions during games. This is reminiscent of the Dutch "Total Football" approach of the 1970s. We are not trying to build teams, but develop individual players, so the development progress of our young players takes priority over team results.

I do think that coaches spend too much on choosing and constantly working on implementing a specific formation. The reality is that if young players do not have a good first touch, accurate passing ability and good technical skills it does really not matter what formation a team plays. The players will struggle during games and likely not enjoy playing them. Similarly if coaches ask players to only play one position, how can that young person develop into a well-rounded player capable of playing all positions later in their career?

As I've recounted earlier, I had a young player try out for the provincial team as a striker. We had a lot of very good strikers and she would not have made the squad if she was not able to adapt to a new position. She became a fullback and went on to captain the team and earn herself a scholarship at a college in the US. Ashley Cole of Chelsea has won 100 caps playing as a fullback for England but started in the Arsenal academy as a left winger. It is important to be flexible rather than rigid with formations and playing positions at the youth levels of the game. Unfortunately, many parents have it in mind that their child "must" play in a certain position and make this a condition of him or her playing on a certain team. This often leads to good players missing out on good coaching opportunities or a spot on stronger teams simply because they will not accept a switch in position.

Top clubs in Europe tend to have their 1st team play in a certain way. For example when I was in Spain at Sevilla FC, the focus of their attacking set-up was their two wingers. Everything came through them to create goal scoring opportunities so at the academy levels much emphasis was placed on ensuring that their youth teams played the same way and that they developed very talented players capable of playing in wide positions. (For example, Jesus Navas, who played on the winning Spain team in the 2010 World Cup and now plays for Manchester City, was a Sevilla wing product.) They tended to play a 4-4-2 formation at the first team level so the youth teams played the same way. I see great benefit in this scenario for playing a specific formation from the youth levels up to the first team so that young players can easily progress through the development system and when asked to play up they will already be familiar with the system of play. However, they don't typically start playing 11 v 11 until age 13 in Spain so there are many years prior to that age where the emphasis should be placed on individual skills development instead of tactics and team formations.

At Wolves, Crewe Alexandra and many of the other academies that I've visited one formation is played and each position (or number) is assigned specific roles and responsibilities. For example the number 4 (central midfielder) would focus on developing certain characteristics such as receiving the ball from defenders, maintaining good possession, making good decisions, tackling, creative passing forward and demonstrating good leadership. In addition, coaches may assign some additional characteristics each week to continually develop the players in all aspects of the game. The coaches do not try to play different formations during the game to achieve winning results but are more focused on developing individual players. As Dario Gradi says at Crewe, "our goal is to develop better players ....and more and more of them."

That aim is not achieved by implementing the formation used by Barcelona or other top clubs throughout the world. The reality is that in most top level games in the world teams change formations two or three times a season to gain tactical advantages. That is because coaches of these teams are tasked with winning games at the professional level. But our role as youth coaches is to develop skillful players with a passion for the game who will be capable of playing at a higher level. Good players in my opinion can play in any formation and they will be asked to play in more than one formation as they progress in the game. During some games they may be asked to change formations two or three times.

My advice to coaches is to focus on developing skills at the youth level and to let the Jose Mourinhos and Arsène Wengers of the world get on with the tactical work at the professional levels of the game. Pick a simple formation or structure for your players to follow and assign them roles and responsibilities for those positions. For players aged 10 and above you can even have them write these down in player books and have them evaluate their own performances based on these objectives after the game. That will encourage them to take more responsibility for their development and enhance their understanding of the game. Talk in terms of roles and responsibilities versus complex and rigid team formations. After all, who cares about game results at the youth levels?

We should be in the development phases for our young players and not trying to go unbeaten for the season.

Made in the USA
Thornton, CO
09/06/22 13:49:08

f3954895-9610-4db2-8cb7-871825125651R01